The Trainer's Tool Kit

Second Edition

Cy Charney
and
Kathy Conway

American Management Association

New York • Atlanta • Brussels • Chicago • Mexico City • San Francisco
Shanghai • Tokyo • Toronto • Washington, D.C.

Special discounts on bulk quantities of AMACOM books are available to corporations, professional associations, and other organizations. For details, contact Special Sales Department, AMACOM, a division of American Management Association, 1601 Broadway, New York, NY 10019.
Tel.: 212-903-8316. Fax: 212-903-8083.
Web site: www.amacombooks.org

This publication is designed to provide accurate and authoritative information in regard to the subject matter covered. It is sold with the understanding that the publisher is not engaged in rendering legal, accounting, or other professional service. If legal advice or other expert assistance is required, the services of a competent professional person should be sought.

Library of Congress Cataloging-in-Publication Data

Charney, Cyril
     The trainer's tool kit / Cy Charney and Kathy Conway.—2nd ed.
       p. cm.
    Includes index.
    ISBN 0-8144-7268-0 (pbk.)
    1. Employees—Training of—Handbooks, manuals, etc. I. Conway, Kathy. II. Title.

    HF5549.5.T7C5412   2005
    658.3'124—dc22

                               2004018328

Printing number

10 9 8 7 6 5 4 3 2 1

Contents

Preface

Expectations about training practices and solutions have changed dramatically in the past few years. Organizations regularly redefine the terms *success* and *performance* to meet evolving client and employee expectations.

At the same time, the number of training options for transferring learning has mushroomed so that e-learning, distance learning, videoconferencing, and self-directed programs are becoming more commonplace as compared with the traditional classroom setting.

The term *training* itself has been broadened to the more inclusive term of *learning*—denoting a broader base of skill-building opportunities through assignments, activities, and focused coaching. This shift has broadened the responsibility for training to include managers, coaches, role models, and mentors as key learning agents. An employee's manager has the ultimate responsibility for supporting and sustaining development. As a result, skill sets for managers reflect this important responsibility.

Many organizations now regard their support for individual development and skills upgrading as competitive advantages in attracting and retaining high performers. The pending retirements of many baby boom employees in the next ten years has necessitated the importance of retaining organizational memory and knowledge management through succession-planning programs. At the same time, a newer generation of workers has been educated and trained differently, thereby requiring training opportunities that are customized to match learning-style preferences. Both the organization and its employees want business-based outcomes that reduce cost.

Training today is typically not measured as a stand-alone process. Measures of success are becoming more focused on training's contribution to—and integration with—other human resource practices. Training must create visible bridges between skills building, core competencies, and performance management. Continuous learning implies that training's mission is not to only close gaps but also to grow organizational capacity by preparing employees for emerging challenges.

Today's trainers (and everyone is a trainer today at some point) inevitably operate in environments that present new challenges and opportunities. Nevertheless, they still must meet standards that have not changed, such as engaging participants, creating an environment that encourages learning, risk taking, practice, and checking for understanding. Most important, trainers must enhance organizational capacity—one trainee at a time.

This book is for them.

Acknowledgments

We would like to thank the following people whose assistance in this revised edition was invaluable:

- Hilary Leighton, Business & Executive Programs Coordinator, University of Northern British Columbia
- Lee Carter, Director, and B. J. Neuman, Program Coordinator, E-Learning Programs, Executive Education Centre, Schulich School of Business, York University, Toronto
- Cory Garlough, Vice President, Global Learning Office, Scotiabank, Toronto
- Don Smith, Senior Vice President, Human Resources, MacKenzie Financial Corporation and Investors Group Inc., Toronto and Winnipeg
- Rosemary Kercz, Office Manager, Charney & Associates Inc.

To my wife, best friend,
great mother and amazing grandmother
Rhona Charney

To my family,
Peter, Katrina, and
Teresa Janecek

I
Training Today

Today's Organizations

> *"The main producers of wealth have become information and knowledge."*
>
> —PETER DRUCKER
> Speaker and Author of *Post-Capitalist Society*

The purpose of an organization is to meet the increasing needs of its stakeholders—customers, management, and staff. To do so, an organization needs to maximize the use of all its resources. Without question, people are an organization's most underutilized asset. Better management practices are vital. Providing people with the tools to perform better is equally important.

- High-performing organizations today need to be able to:
  - ✓ Identify and grow the pool of talent interested in, and available for, new opportunities
  - ✓ Encourage employees to learn new skills that will equip them to better handle new challenges
  - ✓ Create roles for managers to facilitate individual career development
  - ✓ Create succession strategies that focus on retention of organizational memory
- High-performing individuals want opportunities to:
  - ✓ Understand the real business of the organization and its impact on their careers
  - ✓ Learn from coaches, role models, and mentors
  - ✓ Create realistic career maps and personalize customized development
  - ✓ Learn and apply skills that are portable and useful
  - ✓ Learn in a manner customized for them
- These factors promote the need for:
  - ✓ Making learning
    - Accessible
    - Spontaneous
    - Affordable
    - Ongoing

✓ Creating multiple knowledge networks
✓ Supporting and rewarding coaches, role models, and mentors who are at the forefront of people development
✓ Linking individual skill building to organizational needs and opportunities
✓ Identifying opportunities for staff to have skill-building opportunities as part of new assignments
✓ Setting standards for pre- and post-training responsibilities for managers and trainers

The role of training is increasingly a shared responsibility among managers, employees, and trainers to identify and ensure the development of new skills. Budgeting for training should not be tied to historical formulas. Rather, it should be linked to the size and urgency of opportunities. At the same time, every training dollar spent must be a business investment. The institutionalization of an individual learning plan in many organizations, for each employee, reflects the recognition that training should be customized to reflect an employee's situation, interests, and opportunities.

Organizational leaders are analyzing training's contribution closely, with business-related measures of quality, timeliness, and cost effectiveness.

This translates into:

• Performing realistic skills assessments
• Choosing the appropriate medium
• Outsourcing as required
• Linking training directly to business objectives
• Listening to managers, employees, and external customers to refine the quality and content of training

Today's Trainers

> *"Those who are successful in the new age are those adept at re-orienting their own and others' activities in untried directions to bring about higher levels of achievement."*

—ROSABETH MOSS KANTER
Harvard Business School Professor and Author

Like trainees, training specialists are not a homogenous group. The training force in an organization has grown to include a corps of subject-matter experts, in-house facilitators, retired specialists, and contract providers. Training specialists may have specialized skills in one or more of the many facets of training design and delivery; however, they are also generalists, capable of organizing training in partnership with others to ensure a good match between need and delivery.

- Effective trainers today typically share some common characteristics for success, including:
  ✓ An appreciation that trainees have various and differed learning styles and preferences
  ✓ An ability to adapt materials and exercises to a targeted population
  ✓ Techniques for gauging whether information has been understood and can be easily applied in the workplace
  ✓ Communication skills that denote respect for a training audience, including listening skills, summarizing, paraphrasing, and effective questioning
  ✓ A commitment to continuous improvement demonstrated by encouraging specific feedback and researching best practices
  ✓ A respect for the diversity of today's labor market and diversity within a training audience
- Group facilitation today requires a broad range of skills. An effective facilitator is able to:
  ✓ Guide participants to arrive at their own conclusions
  ✓ Draw on the group's expertise, knowledge, and experience

✓ Adjust strategies and approaches to meet the learner's needs
✓ Describe and discuss behavioral models
- Trainers need continuous feedback about:
  ✓ Influencing diverse audiences
  ✓ Consulting with business leaders
  ✓ Gathering and acting on meaningful feedback
  ✓ Setting personal development goals
- When communicating with others in a learning environment, no trainer can be successful without meeting the following three key principles:
  1. Demonstrated commitment to—and enthusiasm for—course content and outcomes
  2. The ability to remain neutral on organizational issues
  3. Respect for adult learners

A trainer who does not follow these rules cannot be a successful trainer.

Today's Trainees

> *"When the student is ready, the teacher will emerge."*
>
> —UNKNOWN

The target training population for any training program or session is no longer a homogenous group, regardless of similarities among the participants' job classification or skills profile. It is becoming increasingly important to consider a training audience as a group of unique individuals who will make their own judgments about training's mission and learning outcomes, and to discover how best to meet individual preferences in group settings.

Today's trainees are influenced by:

- *Prior Learning Experiences.* Today's learners, especially newer entrants to the labor market, have been educated differently. Many college and university courses rely heavily on online technology, distance learning, and group assignments. Within organizations, classroom learning is often supplemented by online assignments and self-directed activities. We may need to prepare trainees for maximizing their learning in the different training media, including the classroom.

- *The Extended Workplace.* The workplace has expanded to encompass many forms of off-site and contract workers, including telecommuters. Training outcomes must consider what the trainee's workplace looks like—who the key contacts are, how one communicates with colleagues and customers, and how success is measured. Training programs that assume a traditional workplace are not relevant for all workers. Also, programs that use enhanced delivery technology should identify resources and contacts for post-course follow-up when on-site coaching is not available.

- *The Value Proposition.* Today's trainees, similar to today's consumers, want to invest time and energy wisely. This means that trainees want effective and relevant training, delivered competently, that justifies the time away from the job. This means paying attention to demonstrating the relationship between skills taught and their application in the workplace for every learning activity and training outcome.

- *Personal Development Goals.* Employees understand that they are largely responsible for managing their own careers. As trainees, they hope to acquire skills that are both relevant and portable, within their organization or others.

- *Diversity.* Diversity among trainees encompasses much more than cultural, religious, and ethnic diversity. Trainees differ in other major ways, including:
  - ✓ Expectations about long-term employment
  - ✓ Desire for upward mobility
  - ✓ Expectations about support they will receive from the organization in terms of pre- and post-training support
  - ✓ Expectations about support for development from immediate managers
  - ✓ Learning skills and learning styles
  - ✓ Preferences for training media and tools
  - ✓ The value and applicability of previous training experiences
  - ✓ Confidence about applying new skills and learning

- *Time-Tested Learning Principles.* While needs and expectations of trainees can change over time, the following adult learning principles have stood the test of time:

✓ They want to learn. They realize that training is a key to their performance and their success. In a world where layoffs are commonplace, people realize that the only things they can take with them to a new job and career are their skills.

✓ They need to be involved and consulted. Letting them know what will be learned, by whom, and when it will be done will increase the buy-in and the commitment to participate enthusiastically.

✓ They want to feel that the content is relevant. They need to feel that the materials have been designed with their special circumstances in mind.

✓ They like to be able to challenge the content and process. Adults need to feel that they can critique ideas frankly.

✓ They enjoy being able to ask questions. The issues that they raise need to be treated seriously and answered within an agreed-upon time.

✓ They like to be treated as equals. No one likes to be talked down to or treated as a child.

✓ They want to be able to practice in a risk-free environment.

✓ They appreciate feedback on how they are doing. Without appropriate validation of their behavior, they may not develop the confidence to repeat the skills that they have learned or correct the skills they performed incorrectly.

✓ They listen actively, confirming the ideas that they agree with and challenging those they disagree with.

✓ They need to be challenged. They should be given tasks that will make them think and behave in ways that will require them to stretch.

✓ People learn differently and work at different rates, because of each person's unique experience, background, ability, and learning styles.

✓ They may need to unlearn old ideas and habits before they can learn something new.

✓ Trainees need to build on their own experiences and knowledge.

✓ They are interested in seeking practical solutions to their problems.

✓ People remember concepts they:
  • Learned most recently

- Heard about more than once
- Were able to practice
- Could implement right away
- Understand are important to know and use
- Are encouraged or rewarded for using by their manger or other important people in the organization

Training Trends—Then and Now

"Education is what survives when what has been learned has been forgotten."

—B. F. SKINNER
Psychologist and Author of *New Scientist*

Training delivery, content, and objectives are influenced by the same dynamics that shape organizational priorities including:

- Employee demographics, including turnover and pending retirements
- Employee learning styles (shaped by education, prior learning experiences, and the new skills they will need)
- Customer demographics, preferences, and expectations
- The competitive landscape (for example, time to market, speed to market, or industry standards)
- Training media options
- Judicious use of training dollars
- Mix of off-site and contract workers

Thus, measures of success for training and learning strategies are evolving, and yesterday's recipe for success may not be valid for today's deliverables. Here are some key shifts that have occurred in the past five years:

Then	**Now**
• training investment per employee	• (training investment per business initiative
• large in-house training departments focused on facilitating and delivering courses	• smaller training departments focused on consulting and recommending action plans
• canvassing employees to develop training needs analyses	• canvassing senior business leaders to assess training needs priorities
• training departments as separate business units	• training departments linked closely with human resources departments and practices
• extensive in-house training curricula	• smaller suite of core courses supported by customized training initiatives as needs emerge
• identifying and measuring *skills* transfer to evaluate training effectiveness	• identifying *skill-to-business* transfer to evaluate training effectiveness
• classroom training as the key learning arena	• the workplace as the key learning arena
• trainers and facilitators as the key learning agents	• coaches, role models, mentors, and subject-matter experts as the key learning agents
• larger classes that reduce cost per participant	• smaller class groups that increase value per participant
• replacing classrooms with on-line learning whenever technologically feasible	• determining the most effective training medium on a course-by-course basis
• pre-course assignments	• post-course learning assignments and action plans
• skills self-assessments conducted *prior to a training course*	• skills self-assessments conducted *before* and *after* a training course

- specific learning outcomes identified for all training courses

- training primarily focused on *closing skills* gaps

- equipping employees for current roles

- 360-degree analysis of employee strengths and weaknesses

- training employees

- head of training a middle manager

- training because we think it is good

- scattered training

- in-house training

- limited scope and responsibility for training department

- specific learning outcomes identified for all workplace assignments

- training focused on *growing skills* to create opportunities

- equipping employees for future roles

- 360-degree analysis of position skills and experience requirements

- training managers to coach employees

- head of learning now a senior executive with the title of chief learning officer

- training because we know it has an impact on performance

- focused training, particularly on leadership development

- outsourced training

- expanded scope to incorporate knowledge management and performance support

Learning Organizations

> *"The ability to learn faster than your competitors*
> *may be the only sustainable competitive advantage."*
>
> —ARIE DE GEUS
> Author and Consultant

A learning organization is one that recognizes the desire of people to learn and grow and provides them with that opportunity to enhance the future of the organization.

- In his groundbreaking book, *The Fifth Discipline*, Peter Senge identified five principles that characterize a learning organization:
  1. Systems thinking
  2. Personal mastery
  3. Mental models
  4. Shared vision
  5. Team learning
- These principles translate into the following three key practices that enable an organization to promote and support continuous learning:
  1. The ability to learn from each other
  2. The ability to learn from personal experience
  3. The ability to learn from the system (that is, organization successes and failures)
- There are three sets of variables that promote or reduce the learning experience:
  1. Conditions
  2. Activities
  3. Results

Conditions

- A learning organization is not created overnight after a sudden shift in management philosophy. It evolves out of a systematic effort to develop a broad range of human resourcing practices.

- Hiring practices must test for demonstrated learning aptitude in the past and enthusiasm about continuous learning.
- Promotion decisions must acknowledge a candidate's contribution to personal and team learning.
- Compensation systems must reward new skill acquisition with incentives that are directly tied to learning practices and results.
- The skills profile of managers includes and stresses coaching and mentoring responsibilities.
- Job design and organization divisions must be reviewed regularly to ensure that staff members understand their roles in contributing to the organization's success.
- Performance measurement systems must identify learning gaps, the opportunities that will flow from bridging the gaps, and the expected intended results after learning has been transferred to the workplace.
- Business plans and organization goals must include the principle of continuous learning as a competitive lever.
- Training tools and courses should include opportunities for informal and self-directed learning.

Activities

- There are many informal activities that create a learning organization—for example:
  - ✓ Continuous feedback—team members to each other, managers to employees, and employees to managers
  - ✓ Open communications practices that encourage suggestions
  - ✓ Opportunities to celebrate successes
  - ✓ Opportunities to share results within and among groups
  - ✓ Regular postmortems about what was done well, what went wrong, and what can be done better
  - ✓ The use of experimentation as a tool for learning
  - ✓ Establishing and refining benchmarks (standards) for all important organization processes
  - ✓ Involving employees in selecting performance measures and evaluating results
  - ✓ Setting goals for teams, as well as individuals
  - ✓ Ensuring that employees have both the information and the tools to maximize their productivity

Results

- Measuring and reporting results is itself a fundamental learning opportunity. To maximize this opportunity, consider the following:
  - ✓ Report important results weekly; use e-mail and voice-mail systems for immediacy.
  - ✓ Hold senior management forums regularly to analyze results; encourage open Q&A with employees.
  - ✓ Communicate results in the context of changing internal, external, and global conditions.
  - ✓ Use charts and diagrams in reporting results.
  - ✓ Recognize successful coaches and mentors in public.
  - ✓ Design learning graphs for key success indicators and measure progress regularly.
  - ✓ Summarize informal and anecdotal feedback about learning outcomes to be included with formal results.

Successful Training Criteria

> *"The great aim of education is not knowledge but action."*
>
> —HERBERT SPENCER
> British Philosopher and Sociologist

Many managers consider training to be expensive, but few consider the cost of poor performance! Although the cost of training can be high, the return on investment will be too, especially if managers follow these principles:

- *Link all training to the goals of the organization.* The organization's documented mission should be referred to at the beginning of all training and reviewed at the end to ensure that the skills learned will enable the trainee to make a direct contribution to the overall organization goal.

- *Get senior-level commitment and involvement.* Line managers provide the rewards and punishments that send signals about what is important and what is not. They can demonstrate their commitment by:
  - ✓ Introducing training sessions
  - ✓ Being available for questions at the end of a session
  - ✓ Following up with participants to ensure that they are putting new skills into practice
  - ✓ Taking courses together with their staff
  - ✓ Rewarding people who are putting new techniques into practice
  - ✓ Role-modeling the key skills
  - ✓ Specifying skills in people's objectives to be included in periodic reviews
- *Train a critical mass of people.* The more important a training course is, the more important it is that people are involved. Putting the majority of key employees through a program sends a strong message about the importance of the program. If the majority of those who attended begin to put the core principles into practice, the culture of the organization will begin to change.
- *Measure and evaluate results.* All expenditures should provide a payback, and training programs need to demonstrate a value to the organization by being evaluated. Measurement invariably leads to improved performance as results are analyzed and opportunities for improvement are uncovered.
- *Maintain a client focus.* No department can operate in a vacuum. Unless the needs of clients are met consistently, the reputation of a training program will deteriorate and program attendance will drop. Internal clients expect their needs to be dealt with quickly and professionally. If costs for programs are charged back to them, they will expect these costs to be competitive.
- *Respect adult-learning principles.* Adults want to be treated as equals by the course leader. They will value training in which they have some control about process and content, work in a safe environment, and enjoy themselves.
- *Use the best resources.* As part of the commitment to making training effective, managers need to use the most effective resources available. Sometimes these are available internally, but often they need to be provided by an outside specialist. There is no point in delivering something homegrown if its entire credibility is put into jeopardy because of poor-quality delivery.

- *Focus on real-world training.* For training to be effective, it needs to be practical and relate to the challenges of the environment to which people will return. Training must go beyond developing awareness and insight to helping people improve their daily performance.
- *Operate within the values of the organization.* The values of the organization must be practiced by those providing the training. Showing respect for people, treating all people equally, being prepared, listening, treating people as adults, and striving for excellence are common values that, if made to take a backseat, will guarantee failure.
- *Involve the target training groups and managers in the program design.* Getting a sample of the audience involved before the workshop will ensure that there is:
  - ✓ Agreement to the content
  - ✓ Enthusiasm for the program
  - ✓ Some shared ownership to ensure a successful outcome

II

Aligning Training with the Organization's Objectives

Training is often seen as an expense; however, the benefits can be significant when training is targeted at skills that are immediately applicable to improving performance. An organization's challenge is to ensure that the training and benefits are in alignment. The focus of Part II is to provide guidance as to how to align training with the skills and trainees that maximize return on investment (ROI).

Linking Training to Business Needs

There is only one measure of training's effectiveness: Did an important change occur that is directly related to an organization's ability to meet its business goals?

- To evaluate training, one can differentiate between programs that teach *skills* and those that convey *information*. Group sessions that deliver information (such as policy changes, statistical information, or organization priorities) are not training sessions; they are communication forums.
- Business-based training links a change in skill level to business objectives. Training outcomes must demonstrate a direct relationship to the following indicators of performance:
  ✓ Quality
  ✓ Timeliness
  ✓ Cost-effectiveness
  ✓ Satisfaction
- Training outcomes can be divided into the following two types of change:
  1. New business challenges
  2. An opportunity to correct business inefficiencies
- Examples of new business challenges include opportunities to:
  ✓ Penetrate new markets
  ✓ Lower production costs
  ✓ Increase the speed of service
- Examples of opportunities to correct business inefficiencies include:
  ✓ A large number of customer complaints
  ✓ Unusually high staff turnover caused by poor management practices
  ✓ Repairs resulting from equipment failure
- Standard courses, such as leadership training and time management, may be about either opportunity or corrections. For example:
  ✓ Leadership training that is intended to increase staff productivity is an *opportunity*. Leadership training that is held as a result of specific employee complaints is a *correction*.

✓ Time-management training that upgrades current skills is an *opportunity*. Time-management training that is in response to deviations from set standards is a *correction*.

- There are four principles for identifying the relationship of training to an organization's needs:
    1. *Understanding the Business Plan.* The business plan refers to organization or department goals that will be either strengthened or compromised by the training.
    2. *Determining Who the Client Is.* The client is the manager who "owns" the business plan and is accountable for its successful implementation.
    3. *Qualifying and Quantifying the Change Required.* The change required is determined by assessing the competence of the trainees and comparing it with the desired performance.
    4. *Assessing the Likelihood That Changes Related to Training Can Be Implemented.* The likelihood is related to specific conditions and factors that will affect the trainees' opportunity to use the new skills.
- A training plan that overlooks any of these four elements cannot demonstrate business-based results, no matter how effective the material or the presentation.
- Business-based training must be prioritized to maximize its impact on an organization's goals.
- The three elements of setting priorities for training are:
    1. *Size of Skill Gap.* The size of the skill gap can be evaluated by determining how much change is needed to meet operational standards.
    2. *Urgency to Close a Skill Gap.* Urgency refers to the deadline for making changes to operating standards through a training initiative.
    3. *Impact of Closing a Skill Gap.* Impact refers to the dollars and time saved or the increased effectiveness that the training initiative can generate.
- When you must make important decisions about what training initiatives should take precedence in your organization, fill out the chart in Exhibit 1 as accurately as you can to aid you in understanding what your training priorities are.

Exhibit 1 will help to identify the situations that have the greatest potential to create significant change. Training one hundred people

Exhibit 1. Priority analysis grid.

Skill Gap	High	Medium	Low
Size			
Urgency			
Impact			

for a low-urgency gap may have significantly less impact than training ten people who can implement significant change quickly.

Aligning Trainers with the Organization

"Education's purpose is to replace an empty mind with an open one."

—MALCOLM FORBES
Art Collector, Author, and Publisher

Trainers' effectiveness can be enhanced significantly when they understand what impact they have on other organizational processes. Trainers themselves can be guilty of viewing a course as an event rather than as a building block in growing talent and capability.

- Design a short course, or series of sessions, that gives trainers the opportunity to learn more about the so-called big picture of developing talent and training priorities. These sessions should include subject-matter experts from other areas. These sessions should:
  ✓ Be practical
  ✓ Avoid rhetoric
  ✓ Encourage two-way dialogue
    - Refer to real-life results and issues
- The components of these sessions should include:
    - *Human Resource Planning.* This discussion should focus on how training is linked with:

- Recruitment criteria
- Selection and promotion decisions
- Performance evaluation
- Core competencies development
- Succession decisions
- Successor development plans
- Career planning support
- 360-degree evaluation
- Formal and informal learning plans
- Formal and informal mentoring programs
- Orientation for new employees

✓ *Training Planning and Budgeting.* Participants should explore whether there are standards for:

- Overall training dollars
- Training days or dollars per employee
- Identifying top training priorities
- Investing in new training technology
- Measuring training against other organizations in your sector or industry
- Evaluating training's impact

✓ *Supporting Managers.* Discussion should revolve around whether there are formal guidelines to help managers:

- Budget and plan for training
- Analyze training needs for their teams
- Select appropriate training courses for employees
- Provide feedback about training courses
- Consult with training specialists about individual development plans

✓ Some sample discussion questions are:

- What incentives or recognition do managers receive for supporting training and learning?
- What drives the bonus structure? (For example, results, 360-degree feedback, retaining employees.)
- Are newly hired recruits or newly promoted employees expected to be fully trained and job ready?
- What are all the formal and informal ways that trainers and human resources specialists exchange information and do joint planning?
- What are the long-term business plans for investing in new training technology? (For example, videoconferencing.)

✓ *Action Plans.* These sessions should include an examination of what kinds of formal and informal feedback trainers require to align key organizational success factors with training objectives. Action plans can focus on:

- Creating focus groups to probe training's effectiveness
- Establishing a cross-functional council to set key deliverables semiannually or quarterly
- Summarizing training results in user-friendly formats
- Shadowing or job exchanges that educate trainers about key jobs in the organization

Training Needs Analysis

"The direction in which education starts a man will determine his future life."

—PLATO

Greek Philosopher and Author of *The Republic*

A training needs analysis refers to the collection and investigation of data about an organization's capability to meet its goals. The *outcome* of a needs analysis is a training action plan to meet a business goal.

- A training needs analysis is:
  - ✓ Based on facts, not assumptions
  - ✓ Directly related to the overall business plan
  - ✓ Time-based (that is, a one- or two-year view)
  - ✓ Tied to core competencies or key success factors for specific roles
  - ✓ Linked directly with other diagnostic tools (for example, performance evaluation, skills inventory, promotion, and turnover statistics)
- A training needs analysis is not:
  - ✓ A developmental wish list for employees or management

✓ Limited to the operational levels; managers and executives should be assessed as well

✓ A commitment for more training and more training courses

- A training needs analysis measures *skills gaps*. A skill is an ability that can:

✓ Bring results

✓ Be measured

✓ Be improved over time

- A gap is the amount of change required to produce a specific result that can be achieved through:

✓ Training

✓ Practice

✓ Feedback

- Training needs analyses are often not useful because they address many factors and activities that training cannot influence, such as market fluctuations. The following steps are a simple method for establishing training priorities:

✓ Identify one key role in any team or unit (*what* is being done).

✓ Identify one important goal for that role (*why* it is being done).

✓ Identify the key skill that supports the goals and the standard set (*how* it is being done).

✓ Measure the gap between the expected standard and current performance. A gap can be positive or negative. Negative gaps are *liabilities*; positive gaps (that is, exceeding standards) are opportunities to set higher standards.

Analyzing the Information

- In Exhibit 2, sixteen employees are performing below the standard, which indicates a training need. Further investigation should be conducted to review:

✓ What kind of training employees have received

✓ What incentives and recognition employees receive when they perform well

✓ What coaching and monitoring takes place

✓ What kind of training best supports "questioning" skills

✓ What format is most effective (for example, self-directed, classroom, et cetera)

Exhibit 2. Prioritizing training needs.

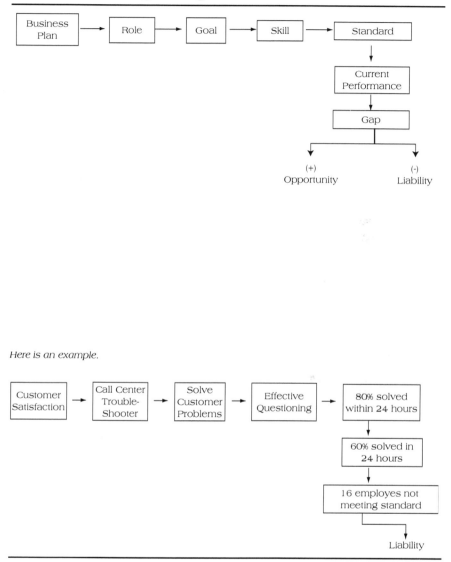

Here is an example.

In the example in Exhibit 2, if employees were exceeding standards, this presents an opportunity to train employees for promotion opportunities or to set higher standards, develop employees for future roles, or to set higher standards that will increase customer retention.

It is important to understand the size of the gap. Small gaps that are liabilities can often be addressed through one-on-one coaching or a refresher session.

The next chapter, "Designing a Training Needs Analysis," provides important guidelines to help managers design and conduct training needs surveys after key gaps are identified.

Designing a Training Needs Analysis

"Planning makes foresight as clear as hindsight."

—UNKNOWN

A training needs analysis will enable managers to anticipate and meet training needs in a timely and cost-effective manner. The following ideas can help ensure that the process is effective and professional:

- A comprehensive training needs survey will contribute to the effectiveness of a training strategy by:
  - ✓ Establishing training priorities
  - ✓ Developing training-budget guidelines
  - ✓ Setting training-delivery deadlines
- To encourage participation in the survey and to solicit useful information, the survey should be:
  - ✓ Anonymous and confidential
  - ✓ Easy to read, with clear instructions and questions
  - ✓ Relevant to the organization's unique operating challenges and conditions
- Use the following guidelines for designing a formal survey:
  - ✓ Use multiple-choice and yes/no questions as often as possible to make it easier and quicker for employees to respond and to collate information.
  - ✓ Ask very specific open questions—for example, about the person's most recent course, most useful course, and most urgent training need.

✓ Leave room for short comments after each major category of questions.
✓ Collect background information about employees, including:
  • Level of education
  • Training history in previous organizations
  • Length of service with the organization
  • Geographic location
  • Major organization division
  • Employee level within the organization (such as executive, manager, or team member)
✓ Determine whether an employee is familiar with key training policies and practices, including:
  • Training catalogs and curriculum
  • Training application forms and course registration procedures
  • Educational assistance programs
  • Performance appraisal system
  • Training library or self-study facility
✓ Use scales for describing a course's usefulness rather than narrative comments.
✓ Limit scales from one to three, to elicit a specific opinion from survey participants.
✓ Differentiate between training needs for proficiency on the job and professional development needs for future positions.
✓ Solicit information about the need for both refresher and new courses.
✓ Do not repeat questions already addressed through post-course evaluations.
✓ Have participants identify specific barriers to training, as well as barriers to practicing skills gained through training.
✓ Use a 360-degree approach to find out what suggestions participants have about their managers' and coworkers' training needs. Include questions about employees' interest in and availability for after-hours training.
✓ Do not assume that all employees are interested in promotion. Ask if, and when, an employee hopes to be promoted.
✓ Rate the effectiveness of other forms of training needs surveys (for example, annual evaluations, managerial coaching, or mentoring).
✓ Ask if employees are willing to contribute to or share the cost of certain kinds of training.

✓ Get information about ideal conditions for training delivery (for example, on-site versus off-site, internal versus external facilitators).

✓ Limit the number of questions. Research demonstrates that the interest and energy level to provide accurate information decrease dramatically after twenty-five questions.

- You may interview a cross-section of managers, particularly the most influential. Ask them the following questions:
  - What are the key performance gaps?
  - Which areas or levels of the organization should be focused on?
  - For ongoing training courses already identified, ask:
    - Who needs the training?
    - How many people need to be trained?
    - What issues should the training resolve?
    - When should the training be complete?
    - How large is the budget?

✓ Once you have collected your information and formulated your plan, meet with key decision makers and present your findings. Your report, oral or in writing, should cover the following topics:
  - The problem
  - The cause
  - Recommended solution
  - Your action plan
  - The cost and benefit
  - Approvals required

Using 360-Degree Feedback for Training Needs Analysis

"Whoso neglects learning in his youth,
loses the past and is dead for the future."

—EURIPIDES
Greek Playwright and Author of *Phrixus*

Typically, 360-degree feedback is the collection and examination of data, observations, and expectations from a variety of sources in order to determine improvements required and the anticipated results.

Good human resource planning links an employee's skills with a specific role. Good training maximizes that fit.

There are many ways to determine what a position, and its incumbent, needs to maximize that fit. Too often, however, we deal in speculation rather than information. Few methods are as effective as the collection of data from:

- Those who rely on the outputs of the position
- Those who can observe the incumbent's performance

The two applications of 360-degree feedback in a training needs analysis are:

1. Position profile
2. Trainee profile

Position Profile

- Conduct a 360-degree investigation of a target position to determine:
  ✓ Key outputs of the role
  ✓ Key internal/external relationships
  ✓ Expectations for the future (such as changes in technology, mandate, client expectations, or population served)

✓ Critical success factors
✓ Threshold experiences and capability
✓ Development time lines
- Involve interviewees such as:
  ✓ Incumbent and previous incumbent
  ✓ Direct reports—current and past
  ✓ Position manager and previous manager
  ✓ Appropriate contacts with benchmarking partners
  ✓ Key internal partners
  ✓ Internal/external customers
- Develop a priority listing of key success skills that:
  ✓ Can be used to determine an incumbent's proficiency
  ✓ Can be measured against objective standards
  ✓ Are consistent with today's requirements and tomorrow's projections
- Develop training action plans that:
  ✓ Link current courses to the needs identified
  ✓ Help managers to select the appropriate trainee audience
  ✓ Customize course content to reflect the 360-degree observations
  ✓ Identify the key learning experiences and coaching a manager will provide after a course or series of courses
  ✓ Set time frames and actions for follow-up

Trainee Profile

There are many ways to determine the key skills a person needs to improve. Gather input from those with whom the individual interacts: the manager, peers, and direct reports. The following steps are a simple way to determine training needs:

- Create a list of skills that courses are intended to improve.
- Develop a survey from the list. The survey could be done in one of two ways:
  1. **An *open-ended survey,*** to allow people to provide a description of how much a particular employee needs to improve on the use of that skill(s) or is effective at using it
  2. **A *numerical ranking*** using a scale of 1 to 10:

1	—	very poor
2.5	—	poor

$$5 \quad - \quad \text{average}$$
$$7.5 \quad - \quad \text{competent}$$
$$10 \quad - \quad \text{very competent}$$

Some surveys use a five-point scale. This is less satisfactory when aggregating the scores of six to ten people who fill out the survey since nuances can be lost that only a larger score will highlight.

- Discuss or communicate the process to each trainee. Clarify important issues such as confidentiality, i.e. who sees the report.
- Give the survey to six to ten people to complete for each potential trainee.
- Make sure that you get a good mix of people—manager, peers, and direct reports—so as not to bias your sample.
- Ensure that the survey is anonymous. Do not ask people to identify themselves by name on the survey.
- Aggregate the data so that all opinions are included.
- Meet with the potential trainee to discuss the report.
- Develop a plan that addresses the trainee's key weaknesses.
- Involve the person's manager (if you are not that person) and mentors (if any) in the training plan. Ensure follow-up and appropriate recognition when trainees finish the program, and also down the road when they meet the goals set for the training.

Core Competencies

Core competencies are descriptions of behaviors and success criteria that are unique to an organization's past and continuing success. The premise of core competencies is that certain skills, attitudes, and role-modeling behavior will predispose individuals to meet goals. This creates a competitive advantage for the organization.

- Core competencies are not a:
  - ✓ Vision or a wish list for success; they are grounded in realistic customer feedback.

- ✓ Training's responsibility; they are integrated into business plans and human resource practices.
- ✓ List of skills; they are descriptions of what a skill "looks like" when practiced and how to recognize opportunities to practice it.
- Core competencies differ by organization and industry. Nevertheless, in all cases, they reflect job content and success in terms of skills, knowledge, and personal characteristics.
- When defined, core competencies are integrated into the following organization practices:
  - ✓ Organization design and restructuring
  - ✓ Job-evaluation systems
  - ✓ Compensation strategy
  - ✓ Performance-measurement criteria and evaluation tools
  - ✓ Recruitment planning
  - ✓ Hiring criteria
  - ✓ Training and development planning
  - ✓ Promotion processes and succession planning
  - ✓ Career planning
  - ✓ Performance evaluation
  - ✓ Productivity analysis
- Core competency profiles for job content and employee success reflect a combination of both "business" competencies and "personal influence" competencies.
- Common business competencies for an organization include:
  - ✓ Personnel management
  - ✓ Financial expertise
  - ✓ Business-plan development and execution
  - ✓ Marketing expertise
  - ✓ Internal and external communications
  - ✓ Policy development and deployment
  - ✓ Sales skills
  - ✓ Customer-relation skills
  - ✓ Project management
- Common personal-influence competencies for an organization include:
  - ✓ Directing work through others
  - ✓ Developing others
  - ✓ Influencing others
  - ✓ Energy and enthusiasm

✓ Working with others
✓ Organization awareness
✓ Analysis and judgment
✓ Adaptability
✓ Change management
✓ Self-confidence
✓ Listening and responding
✓ Perseverance
✓ Consistency

- Training and development professionals and line managers will be working more closely together than ever before in organizations that have developed core competencies. Together, they are refining training course content and selecting participants who will model the core competencies.

- The following opportunities can link core competencies with training and learning initiatives:

  ✓ Highlight specific skills in internal training courses that strengthen a specific competency.

  ✓ Arrange for presentations during training courses by recognized role models in a specific competency; presentations should include a question-and-answer period to discuss specific on-the-job scenarios.

  ✓ Develop a coaching course for managers that focuses specifically on coaching for competency development.

  ✓ Select mentors for formal programs based on demonstrated excellence in specific competencies and partner them with mentees who wish to develop that competency.

  ✓ Build core competencies into training needs analyses and surveys.

  ✓ Highlight core-competency development in case studies and exercises.

Developing a Training Curriculum

> *"The whole art of teaching is only the art of awakening the natural curiosity of young minds for the purpose of satisfying it afterwards."*
>
> —ANATOLE FRANCE
> French Novelist, Storyteller, and Author of *The Crime of Sylvestre Bonnard*

A training curriculum is a road map, or planning tool, that sets out some key courses and related policies that help employees meet and exceed performance standards. It typically comprises approved courses—offered both internally and externally—that are mandatory, or recommended, for certain common roles or functions. These course offerings will change over time as organizational priorities shift.

- A training curriculum benefits both managers and employees because of the following reasons:
  - ✓ It underscores an organization's support for skill development and continuous learning.
  - ✓ It creates common learning experiences for employees in similar roles.
  - ✓ Managers can prepare employees before, and debrief them after, standard courses.
  - ✓ It encourages advance planning and budgeting for training.
  - ✓ Quality control and feedback can be monitored and corrected.
  - ✓ Managers and employees can refer to the curriculum to create development plans during performance discussions and evaluation meetings.
- A training curriculum should reflect overall business planning and feedback from managers about development needs for individuals and teams. A curriculum should have a balanced mix of courses that will:
  - ✓ Equip people to adapt to their current job
  - ✓ Enhance personal effectiveness in any job—for example, negotiation or presentation skills
  - ✓ Prepare people to advance to another level

- It is not necessary to address *all* training needs and options in a curriculum; however, each course that is included in the curriculum should contain information about the following:
  - ✓ Learning objectives
  - ✓ Learning outcomes
  - ✓ Eligibility criteria
  - ✓ Summary of feedback and observations from previous participants
- A curriculum can be divided into broad training categories, such as:
  - ✓ Leadership and influencing skills—for example, feedback or coaching
  - ✓ Personal effectiveness skills—for example, time management or project management
  - ✓ Sales and customer service—for example, handling objections or marketing
  - ✓ Equipment and technology
- Within each of these categories, there are typically courses that are:
  - ✓ Mandatory
  - ✓ Recommended
  - ✓ Optional
- Mandatory courses are tied directly to performance standards or quality guidelines. Organizations should budget and administer these centrally to ensure equal access for all eligible employees.
- A published training curriculum should be available to all employees. This publication should also include information about:
  - ✓ The role of the manager and the employee in making training decisions
  - ✓ Application procedures
  - ✓ Self-directed resources
  - ✓ Supplemental resources materials (for example, books, videos, or catalogs)
  - ✓ Mentoring programs
- Employees who attend external training courses can provide important information for others considering a course. Exhibit 3 contains a sample questionnaire that employees can complete. This information is a useful supplement to a training curriculum.

Exhibit 3. Sample follow-up feedback form.

Training Effectiveness Follow-Up

Thank you for your time and interest in helping other employees make important decisions about effective use of training opportunities.

Course Name:	Location (city):	
Provider:	Course length (days):	
Cost:	Class size:	

How did you hear of this course?

☐ Literature	☐ Core curriculum	☐ Personal recommendation
☐ Industry/professional association	☐ Your manager	☐ Other (specify)

Was this training topic (check one):

☐ Recommended by your manager	☐ Self-identified

Course format (check all that apply):

☐ Learning & practicing new skills	☐ Information only	☐ Information & case studies
☐ Group exercises	☐ Highly discussion-oriented	☐ Other (specify)

Participants (check one):

❑ Performing similar duties as yours	❑ Different positions than yours	❑ Combination of both

When will you apply the skills (check one):

❑ Immediately	❑ 6 months to one year	❑ At an undetermined future date	❑ Unlikely to apply

Professionalism (indicate H-M-L):

Facilitator	Materials	Lessons learned

Cost effectiveness (check one):

❑ Very good value . . . worth more than the cost	❑ Didn't justify the cost
❑ Justified the cost	❑ Not worth it at any cost

Will you discuss this training with your manager?	❑ Yes ❑ No
Would you recommend this course to others?	❑ Yes ❑ No

III
Maximizing the Training Investment

Getting value for money and operating within budget is not just the purview of line managers and the finance department. It is also a key requirement of training professionals, who need to be seen as full business partners.

Budgeting for Training

"He that is of the opinion money will do everything may well be suspected of doing everything for money."

—INVENTOR BENJAMIN FRANKLIN

Too often training plans and budgets sit on a shelf as circumstances and priorities change. Training that does take place may have little to do with what was planned. When training budgets are ignored, training's relationship to the success of the organization may be questioned.

The following guidelines can help ensure that training budgets and plans address real business concerns:

- Break budget projections into the following four key categories:
  1. *Organization Skill Gaps*—Training that supports mandatory changes in the business plan, including new products, services, and technology
  2. *Turnover Gaps*—Training that supports employee orientation to the organization or to a new business unit
  3. *Individual Skill Gaps*—Training that is unique to an individual's performance
  4. *Strategic Change Gaps*—Training to facilitate a new direction or to promote a change in culture
- Understand the business plans *before* developing your own plan for training. Linking the two will provide the greatest benefit to the organization.
- Research the best method for budget projections for your organization, considering the following sources:
  ✓ Competitor research
  ✓ Organizations with the same employee base
  ✓ Government research
  ✓ Industry and association research
  ✓ Recruitment plans
  ✓ Retirement projections
  ✓ Product upgrades
  ✓ Equipment upgrades

- Before building detailed training plans, determine the maximum amount of resources your organization will invest, keeping in mind all the considerations previously outlined.
- Use any number of the most common methods of creating a training budget, such as:
  - ✓ Commit a set percentage for training based on overall salary expenditures.
  - ✓ Commit a set percentage for training based on overall anticipated organization revenue.
  - ✓ Establish a standard number of days per employee for professional development.
  - ✓ Prioritize training needs that are articulated in the business plan and estimate the associated costs.
  - ✓ Use historical information about training costs. Adjust these costs for inflation and changes in the number of employees.
  - ✓ Total all cost estimates submitted by individual line managers. Then subtract the current figure for all salaries from the total amount of salaries that would be owing if all employees were paid at the maximum allowable level.
  - ✓ Use figures from government agencies and professional associations to set your organization's guidelines.
- Once the skill gaps have been identified, perform the following analyses:
  - ✓ Differentiate between "must do" and "nice to do" priorities.
  - ✓ Establish the total budget commitment for each category.
  - ✓ Determine the total amount of employee time off the job that can be guaranteed for training purposes.
  - ✓ Determine the best training courses or tools that will fit the dollar and time allocations for priority skill gaps.
  - ✓ Add to the costs of courses the costs of trainee travel, training facilities, and printed resource material.
  - ✓ Allocate a contingency cost for unexpected business plan changes. Use a guideline of 10 percent of the total of the previous costs.
- The grid shown in Exhibit 4 can be used to reexamine your organization's costs and anticipated benefits and perhaps to realign monies and delivery options.
- The grid shown in Exhibit 5 can be used to help identify your organization's most urgent training needs when considering the best training solutions to meet those needs.

Exhibit 4. Training priority grid.

Training Need	Skill Gap (check one—X)			Business Impact (check one—X)			Priority Ranking	Training Solution
	High	Med.	Low	High	Med.	Low		

Exhibit 5. Sample of a training priority grid.

Training Need	Skill Gap (check one—X)			Business Impact (check one—X)			Priority Ranking	Training Solution
	High	Med.	Low	High	Med.	Low		
Orientation training for 25 newly recruited sales reps		X			X		2	Product overview training
Management training for 10 new supervisors		X		X			1	Corporate leadership program
Customer service training for technicians	X					X	3	Purchase XYZ course from KLM vendor

(In this chart, the reasons for the rankings are as follows for this fictitious company:)

The liability of untrained supervisors is considered the greatest need because of their inexperience and their effect on employee morale. Although the product knowledge for sales reps is a mandatory requirement, there are other methods available for them to learn the products—brochures and access to seasoned sales reps. The customer service training for technicians is a new business opportunity that will enhance the company's public relations profile, with a long-term objective of increasing sales.

Although each training project has an important impact on the business, it is critical to differentiate the magnitude of each impact.

Budgets: Building a Case for More Training Dollars

M ost organizations today find themselves in a catch-22 situation about training. There is an increased need for training to provide help for employees challenged to meet changing market conditions. At the same time, there are limited funds because of budget restrictions.

Making a case for more training dollars requires research and data from many sources. A comprehensive analysis about the requirement for more training dollars should focus on the following:

- Business-plan liabilities
- Benchmarking
- Customer and employee feedback

Business-Plan Liabilities

- Your organization's twelve-month business plan should outline key initiatives that are critical to its success. Many of these initiatives assume the availability of competent and trained staff. The business plan can be jeopardized if staff is not trained in areas such as:
  ✓ New equipment startup
  ✓ New or enhanced information technology
  ✓ Maintenance and repair of older equipment
  ✓ Features and benefits of new products
  ✓ Updated research about customer attitudes and expectations
  ✓ New legislation affecting manufacturing processes, safety standards, workplace conditions, and employee relations
- Prepare a situation analysis that describes the current operating capability for meeting these new requirements. Any skills shortfall that is not in the training plan should be highlighted, costed, and presented to management as a key condition for meeting planning projections.
- In any operating environment, there are other liabilities attached to

limiting training. These risks are often not seen as training issues—until it is too late. Be on the lookout for the following signals:

✓ Unusually high staff turnover, often caused by inexperienced or untrained managers
✓ Delays in meeting customer delivery deadlines
✓ Customer complaints about product defects and not meeting service standards
✓ Equipment breakdown
✓ Billing mistakes and invoicing errors
✓ Missed production targets

- Training is not the solution for all these problems, but there may be a relationship between training and performance standards in past records. In documenting these relationships, compare the costs of inefficiencies to the costs of training, and set priorities for using training dollars where the benefits clearly outweigh the costs.
- Be sure to include an analysis of the availability of qualified, trained staff to replace employees who leave. External recruiting and on-site orientation are expensive.

Benchmarking

- Draw on the many sources of information that can help you to determine a reasonable training investment for your organization. Gathering this information should be an ongoing activity. The following sources can be accessed readily:
  ✓ Professional training associations that provide data about training costs, broken down by organization size and type.
  ✓ Government agencies that collect data about industrywide training expenditures (such as training costs or training days).
  ✓ Industry and trade associations, which often conduct surveys to benchmark training costs.
  ✓ Your own organization. With a little research, you can analyze annual changes to the training budget and compare them with changes in employee population and business-plan achievement.
  ✓ Consultants who work with your organization often have interesting observations about overall trends for training investments.
- When presenting your research, be sure to include all associated costs of training, including the following:

✓ Training-staff salaries
✓ Multimedia equipment
✓ Outsourcing
✓ Reference materials
✓ Travel and accommodation costs

- Break down all associated costs, and pinpoint which ones can contribute to greater efficiencies and economies of scale.

Customer and Employee Feedback

- Customer and employee feedback can provide compelling evidence for the need for increased training investments. Use the following tools to gather meaningful feedback and ongoing needs analyses:
  ✓ Employee attitude surveys
  ✓ Information about training practices and needs gained during exit interviews
  ✓ Records to help you track the number of employees hired externally over a period of time due to a lack of qualified internal candidates
  ✓ Employee focus groups
  ✓ Customer focus groups
  ✓ Customer complaint logs
  ✓ Customer satisfaction surveys
  ✓ Feedback from sales and customer service representatives

Costs and Benefits of Training

"Only the educated are free."

—EPICTETUS
Roman Philosopher, Slave, and
Author of *Discourses*

Most organizations would like to be able to measure the costs invested in training initiatives against anticipated results. The challenge is that it is far easier to measure the costs of conducting training than it is to quantify results. A useful tool in determining costs and savings is to compare costs per participant versus savings per participant.

Comparing costs and benefits can be done in the following four simple steps:

1. *Calculate the cost of training.* This will include training costs such as:
   ✓ Facilitator fees
   ✓ Training design
   ✓ Course materials
   ✓ Videos and workbooks
   ✓ Facilities rental
   ✓ Equipment rentals (such as overhead projectors)
   ✓ Production downtime (including employee time off the job)
   ✓ Videoconferencing facilities
   ✓ Specialized computer equipment
   ✓ Administration (such as registration procedures or confirmation notices)
   ✓ All the relevant costs, divided by the anticipated number of participants, gives the cost per participant.
2. *Determine the potential savings generated.* These savings might include:
   ✓ Fewer errors
   ✓ Reduced customer turnover
   ✓ Less equipment downtime
   ✓ Increased revenue collection
   ✓ Faster equipment start-up time
   ✓ Reduced employee turnover, when turnover is attributable to poor supervision
   ✓ Proper implementation of new customer strategies
   ✓ Higher workplace morale through more effective management practices
   ✓ Less time lost to grievance hearings and work stoppages because of ineffective supervision
   ✓ Reduced recruitment costs (because training can create more job-ready candidates for promotions)
   ✓ Maximized productivity of new employees through efficient orientation training

3. *Calculate the potential savings.* To calculate potential savings, set goals for post-training achievements by identifying and quantifying the changes a training initiative will produce if all other factors are constant. The factors in the formula include the following:
   ✓ Current level of performance (for example, 200 error rates per month; 6 lost customer accounts per month; 5 days lost to work stoppages per year).
   ✓ Translate the current level of performance into a dollar figure. For example:

$$200 \text{ error rates} \times 5 \text{ minutes correction time} \times \$15 \text{ salary per hour} = \$250 \text{ per month}$$

   ✓ Identify the change that training can produce (for example, reduce errors to 50 per month
   ✓ Calculate the savings that the target criteria will generate. For example:

$$200 \text{ errors} - 50 \text{ errors} = \text{decrease of 150 errors per month savings} = 150 \times 5 \text{ minutes}/60 \times \$15 = \$187.50$$

   ✓ Identify a meaningful time line for realizing savings, based on your best business predictions about factors contributing to errors remaining unchanged.
   ✓ Identify the number of employees in the target training group.
   ✓ Divide the total anticipated savings by the number of participants to identify the savings per participant.
4. *Compare the costs to savings.*
   ✓ Multiply the cost per participant by the total number of participants.
   ✓ Multiply the savings per participant by the total number of participants.
   ✓ Compare your figures to establish your business case for training.

This exercise not only identifies actual costs and realistic savings but also ensures that your training expectations are reasonable and targeted to measurable business outcomes.

Alternatives to Training

Organizations want to find the fastest, most realistic way of closing a knowledge or skill gap. Do an upfront needs analysis to make sure that training is the answer.

- Training cannot close a skill gap that is caused by:
  - ✓ Poor morale or attitude
  - ✓ Poor policies or procedures
  - ✓ Equipment problems
  - ✓ Lack of incentives
- Training may not be the fastest solution for closing a skill gap when:
  - ✓ The time to develop and deliver the training cannot meet new skill implementation deadlines.
  - ✓ Employee time off the job to attend training will result in decreased productivity.
  - ✓ Work shifts and holiday schedules necessitate training small groups at one time, over a long period of time.
- Training may not be the most realistic solution for closing a skill gap when:
  - ✓ There are only a few employees affected by a new skill requirement.
  - ✓ The need for new skills is only short term.
  - ✓ Costs of a course are higher than the benefits the training will produce.
  - ✓ Regular training courses are poorly attended.
  - ✓ Courses convey information only, not skill building.
- The following alternatives to training can close skill gaps:
  - ✓ Change hiring and promotion criteria to reflect new skill requirements.
  - ✓ Pay higher salaries for some positions to attract job-ready employees.
  - ✓ Institute job-shadowing programs.
  - ✓ Set up formal mentor programs.
  - ✓ Implement job rotations for hands-on practical experience.
  - ✓ Set up buddy systems with retired employees.

✓ Recognize and reward managers who are effective coaches.

✓ Set up individual development plans for employees whose performance is unsatisfactory.

✓ Create self-service employee learning resource centers, which provide training materials that people can borrow.

✓ Develop user-friendly, self-paced, how-to manuals and job aids for common problems.

✓ Establish help lines for equipment- and technology-related problems.

✓ Designate experienced employees as troubleshooters for specialized problems.

✓ Put together a list of employees with specialized skills and training who can provide individual assistance.

✓ Hold cross-functional meetings for employees to share their expertise.

✓ Set aside time in regular meetings for employees to brainstorm problems and coping techniques.

✓ Invite industry experts to participate in information panels.

✓ Design a tuition reimbursement program for job-related education.

✓ Reimburse employee purchases of job-related books and videos.

• Training is especially ineffective and expensive when it is used:

✓ To train large groups of people in order to correct the behavior of only a few.

✓ To inspire or motivate employees. Only good management practices and meaningful compensation strategies can do that.

✓ To correct fundamental hiring errors.

✓ To encourage employees to market or sell products that the customers don't want.

✓ To solve disciplinary problems. These are one-on-one situations.

✓ To reduce employee turnover or absenteeism. Working conditions are usually the culprit here.

• Employee input and feedback are often the best source of suggestions for cost-effective alternatives to expensive training. Put their resourcefulness to work for you.

Stretching the Training Dollars

A training course that has high-priority impact shouldn't be abandoned because of an apparent high cost. The following measures can reduce total costs so that key training interventions aren't shelved:

- Train key participants, and use them as coaches for others.
- Break down course material into modules to reduce the strain on daily operations.
- Reduce lengthy courses to key teaching points, and supplement them with videos and books.
- Set up partnerships with other organizations to share the costs of common training courses.
- Seek out government grants or industry association support for costs.
- Split the costs of training with participants for personal development courses.
- Negotiate with consultants for approval to reproduce training manuals in-house.
- Negotiate volume discounts with consultants.
- Conduct training after hours or on weekends.
- Apply penalties to no-show scheduled trainees where costs are incurred to run the program.
- Use in-house subject matter experts as facilitators.
- Share costs with unions or other employee associations.
- Explore lower-cost training provided through local colleges and universities.
- Conduct training on site rather than at expensive hotels or conference facilities.
- Trade training sites with local organizations.
- Set up volume discounts with airlines and hotels to reduce travel expenses.
- Arrange lower consultant costs in exchange for free publicity.
- Co-venture a new training program with a vendor. You get unlimited access; the vendor gets the copyright.

- Put together a group of organizations with similar needs for volume discounts or to fund all-new design.
- Travel costs for trainees and facilitators can be significant. They can even lead to delays or cancellation of important training projects. Use the following tips for reducing these costs:
  ✓ Videotape important sessions so that employees who cannot attend scheduled courses can understand the key teaching points. This is more cost-effective than makeup sessions.
  ✓ Set realistic limits for meals and incidental expenses during travel.
  ✓ Start training courses at noon so that out-of-town employees can save the cost of a hotel room the night before the session.
  ✓ For some training courses, videoconferencing can be a cost-effective alternative. If your organization does not have its own facilities, explore the possibility of renting facilities at a local college or university.
  ✓ Provide incentives (such as dinner coupons or theater tickets) for employees to stay with friends or relatives during training at an out-of-town location.

Using Consultants

> *"Competence, like truth, beauty and contact lenses, is in the eye of the beholder."*
>
> —LAURENCE J. PETER
> Canadian Teacher and Author of *The Peter Principle*

For every consulting success story, there's a story about poor service, outrageous prices, and dashed expectations. The availability of consulting firms and independent entrepreneurs presents greater choices than ever before. At the same time, checking credibility can be a challenge, yet no organization can afford poor service.

- Consultants provide several advantages:
  ✓ Up-to-date training expertise in specialized areas

   ✓ Lower-cost solutions for repeated training needs or for one-time-only initiatives
   ✓ Different perspectives
   ✓ Labor-market information gained from working with other organizations
   ✓ Responsiveness to meet tight deadlines
   ✓ Skills and programs that are not available in-house
- Some disadvantages in dealing with consultants are that they:
   ✓ Have less commitment to an organization's long-term success
   ✓ Cost more, on an hourly basis, than internal training staff
   ✓ Work for your competitors too and may jeopardize confidentiality
   ✓ May not have an in-depth appreciation of your organization's culture
   ✓ Will want to be paid no matter how successful (or unsuccessful) the initiative is
- Managers are bombarded with calls from consultants offering their services. Use the following suggestions for managing a high volume of unsolicited calls:
   ✓ *Never* be rude. You represent your organization at all times, and any bad manners on your part reflect on your organization.
   ✓ Request literature from consultants before agreeing to a meeting. This material will give you a sense of the professionalism of the consultant and client references.
   ✓ Designate one afternoon a month to meet with prospective consultants.
   ✓ Mail out copies of your organization's training catalog to callers. This will save time on both sides so that consultants don't pitch for programs that you already have.
   ✓ Prepare a semiannual summary of your training needs to send to callers so that you will hear back only from those who are able to meet your requirements.
   ✓ Designate a junior training employee to meet with callers to screen those who may meet your needs.
   ✓ Ask callers about their industry expertise, client references, and training credentials.
   ✓ Ask callers about their perspective on training trends and organization challenges to gain a sense of their experience.
   ✓ Meet with some consultants from time to time. They bring information about the marketplace.

✓ Keep all literature you receive from consultants during the year. This is an excellent source of competitive information and research.

- Before hiring a consultant, ask the following questions:
  ✓ How good is the consultant's reputation? You don't judge a book by the cover, so don't base your evaluation on the slickness of the consultant's brochures or presentation.
  ✓ How did the consultant contact you? Was it a reference or a cold call?
  ✓ What makes the consultant uniquely qualified to help you with the particular challenge you have?
  ✓ How credible are the consultant's references?
  ✓ How similar have the consultant's other assignments been to your own, and how effective has the training been?
- During an interview meeting with a consultant, establish:
  ✓ What makes his service special? What innovative work has the consultant done?
  ✓ Whether the consultant is using your organization as a test site for a new program.
  ✓ What written materials will be made available to the trainees? Will they be customized?
  ✓ How flexible the consultant is about specific issues you have about costs, numbers of trainees, and the time of training (evenings, weekends, etc.).
  ✓ Whether the consultant will provide you with a written outline of the program, including course objectives.
  ✓ How the effectiveness of the training will be measured.
  ✓ If any guarantees about improvement are given in measurable formats.
  ✓ The professional qualifications and experience of the trainer who will be working on your assignment.
  ✓ The personality and motivational style of the trainer. Given the culture of your organization, will that style fit?
  ✓ How flexible the trainer is in terms of course duration and course content. (Short, punchy modules over a period of time are more effective than lengthy three-day workshops.)
  ✓ Whether your staff will have a direct hotline to the trainer whenever they need support or advice.
  ✓ What homework the consultant has done about your organiza-

tion in terms of size, market niche, competitive edge, and product lines.
- ✓ How competitive the fee structure is compared with others in the field.
- ✓ Whether the quoted prices are inclusive, or whether there are additional costs for duplication of materials, travel, and other items.
- ✓ If and how often the consultant speaks at high-profile conferences.
- ✓ Whether the consultant has published articles in respected journals or newspapers.
- ✓ Whether the consultant does work for any government. (Governments are very strict in qualifying consultants.)
- ✓ If the trainer has backup in the event of sickness or other emergency for a scheduled training course date.
- ✓ If the consultant belongs to any recognized professional associations.
- ✓ How long the consultant has been in business.
- ✓ Relevant experience in your industry.
- Despite your best efforts, there may be occasions that leave you feeling that your money was spent poorly and time was wasted. Examples of poor investments include:
  - ✓ The majority of trainees considered the training a waste of time.
  - ✓ You paid a premium price for a poor product.
  - ✓ The consultant's conduct was unprofessional and resulted in complaints.
  - ✓ Promised workbooks and videos for the session were not available.
- Here are some follow-up techniques that can minimize the impact of a consultant's poor performance:
  - ✓ Negotiate for a reduced fee for the work already done.
  - ✓ Negotiate for reduced fees for upcoming initiatives.
  - ✓ Ask the consultant to prepare a recovery strategy at no extra cost.
  - ✓ Ask the consultant to stage a free "lunch-and-learn" seminar.
  - ✓ Review trainee evaluations with the consultant as a mutual learning opportunity.
  - ✓ Apologize to trainees for any inappropriate or insensitive remarks the consultant made. Make it clear that this is not the organization's way of doing things!

✓ If you generally like the services of the consulting firm and are disappointed with one specific representative, ask for a replacement for the rest of the project.

✓ Explain your follow-up strategies to disappointed trainees.

✓ Do research and trainee follow-up to determine whether you are reacting to the opinions expressed by only a few malcontents.

✓ For long-term projects, pay a penalty fee to discontinue the initiative rather than hoping for the best if initial reviews are poor.

✓ Use every poor consulting experience as an opportunity to understand your role in setting realistic expectations.

- Consultants have rights too. It is difficult for them to be successful when organizations don't deliver the information or access to background material that was promised. Changing delivery dates, canceling meetings, or delaying payments is unprofessional—and it is behavior that you would never tolerate in a consultant.

Outsourcing

Organizations everywhere are focusing resources and energy on managing their core businesses and are finding it more economical to outsource some activities to specialists who can demonstrate quality, delivery, and cost competitiveness.

- Organizations outsource a variety of training activities, including the following:
  ✓ Specialized course development
  ✓ Specialized course delivery
  ✓ Training needs analysis
  ✓ Training facilities
  ✓ Designing information systems that track training statistics
  ✓ Training administration
- Outsourcing some or all training activities should be considered if any of the following conditions exist for your organization:

✓ Demand for training fluctuates during the year and from year to year.
✓ In-house expertise cannot meet some specialized training requirements.
✓ A specific training need is a onetime-only occurrence.
✓ The ongoing costs of an in-house training department become difficult to justify.
✓ There is a high rate of no-shows for your training courses, which can imply that the curriculum is not relevant to the organization's challenges.
✓ Training-department staff members are often deployed to other functions to meet operational needs.
✓ Your organization is spending significantly more than similar-size organizations for the same amount of training.

- Outsourcing has a number of advantages, including:
  ✓ Reduced overhead costs
  ✓ A direct relationship between training needs and training costs
  ✓ Meaningful cost-benefit analysis applied to training requirements
  ✓ Focused expectations for results, based on expenditures
  ✓ A wider selection of qualified professionals to meet organization needs
  ✓ The ability to terminate unproductive consulting relationships
  ✓ Better ability to use the latest methodology and training techniques
  ✓ Greater competitiveness by using current information
  ✓ Accurate tracking of training costs
  ✓ Reduced administrative costs incurred in managing training
  ✓ Just-in-time delivery for important initiatives
- The disadvantages of outsourcing include the following:
  ✓ Typically higher costs for outsourcing on a project-by-project basis
  ✓ The use of consultants who may not understand your business plan
  ✓ The use of consultants who are not as committed to your corporate objectives as in-house training staff may be
  ✓ Confusion generated in your employee population by a multiplicity of messages and biases from consultants
  ✓ Reliance on consultants' availability for scheduling delivery dates

✓ No on-site availability of internal training consultants for impromptu meetings about training requirements
✓ Time-consuming research about prospective consultants and meetings and interviews with them
✓ Training initiatives that may not be linked easily to your organization's recruitment, promotion, and career-development strategies
✓ Potential breaches of confidentiality with respect to important corporate strategies
- Each organization makes its own decisions about the cost-effectiveness of outsourcing, depending on the availability and cost of internal training staff. When outsourcing does occur, the cost-benefit analysis should be reviewed regularly in light of changing business variables.

Choosing Facilities

C lassroom training can be conducted on or away from an organization's premises. The following guidelines can help you find the best venue.

Making the Choice

The following list includes items that all good sites should have:

- Nearby restrooms
- A telephone number for messages for participants
- Message board
- Nearby breakout rooms
- Adequate coatracks
- Access to good equipment (flip charts, markers, wall space to put flip charts, etc.)

- Lighting controls
- Electrical outlets placed conveniently for equipment usage
- Coffee service table
- Trash containers
- Comfortable chairs and tables
- Public transportation access
- Adequate parking
- Handicap access
- Transportation arrangements to and from local airports
- Early-morning access
- Proximity to a variety of good eating places

Costs

Costs will vary depending on your needs. When you've decided on a venue, ensure that there are no surprises by determining whether the following costs are covered in the "package":

- The room
- Equipment rental
- Coffee and lunch service
- Breakout rooms
- Cancellation penalty
- Discounts for trainees who are staying overnight in the facility
- Volume discounts for frequent use
- Facilities

Alternative Facilities

Using hotels for off-site training can be expensive. Consider the following lower-cost alternatives:

- Organization boardrooms and conference rooms
- Local educational institutions
- Boards-of-trade facilities
- Vendor training facilities
- Training rooms in other organizations
- Government facilities (for example, city hall)

- Industry association facilities
- Professional association facilities
- Public libraries

Urge your staff to be creative in suggesting training sites. For example, consider holding workshops in different employee homes when you have a smaller group. The host can be rewarded with a floral arrangement and all food left over from the luncheon buffet. The trainers enjoy a comfortable learning environment while enjoying the hospitality of a team member.

Requests for Proposals for Training Services

Many organizations use requests for proposal (RFPs) when contracting training services. These are formal documents that set out criteria and specifications for training projects. Organizations may invite selected vendors to bid for the project or publicize the RFP in an open forum, such as a trade journal.

- The advantages of using an RFP for training services are:
  - ✓ Expectations for the project are clear.
  - ✓ Proposals from vendors are in a consistent format.
  - ✓ Comparing vendors against common criteria enhances decision making.
- RFPs are most commonly used for the following reasons:
  - ✓ The project is extensive in terms of size, budget, and impact.
  - ✓ A organization's administrative procedures stipulate that all contracts over a set price must be put to bid.
  - ✓ A number of people will be involved in the decision.
  - ✓ The decision makers do not have in-depth knowledge of the products and services available in the marketplace.
- It is difficult to choose among many competent vendors. However,

it is in the organization's best interest to be perceived as fair and equitable in awarding contracts.
- RFPs can include as many criteria as deemed important. At a minimum, all RFPs should include:
  - ✓ A clear description of the project and anticipated outcomes
  - ✓ The number of employees to be trained
  - ✓ Deadline date for the receipt of a completed RFP
  - ✓ Deadline date for the completion of the project
- State your expectations clearly in your RFP. You may even invite vendors to make recommendations for criteria, which typically include:
  - ✓ Pricing
  - ✓ Deliverables, including workshop objectives
  - ✓ Project evaluation criteria
  - ✓ Meetings with the organization
  - ✓ Materials (for example, workbooks and handouts)
  - ✓ Invoicing and payment guidelines
- The following additional vendor information in the completed RFP can help the decision-making process:
  - ✓ Organization background
  - ✓ Financial statements
  - ✓ Facilitator profiles
  - ✓ Client profiles and references
  - ✓ Professional accreditation
  - ✓ Sample materials, such as workbooks
- Sometimes special circumstances should be noted in the RFP, for example:
  - ✓ The need for training in a second language, such as French or Spanish
  - ✓ Potential conflicts of interest (some organizations require vendors to declare any family relationships in the organization)
  - ✓ A requirement for potential vendors to declare current or recent contracts with competitors
- In choosing a format for your RFP, consider the following options:
  - ✓ A standard form already used by your organization for awarding contracts.
  - ✓ An adaptation of a form used by your organization.
  - ✓ An adaptation of a form developed for training contracts used by other organizations.
  - ✓ The time, research, and energy that vendors invest in respond-

ing to RFPs can be extensive. Some organizations pay a small fee to vendors for completed proposals as an acknowledgment of the investment. Although not common, this practice demonstrates your commitment to effective decision making based on comprehensive information.

- The following guidelines can be used by consultants responding to an organization's request for proposal:

  ✓ Use your network to discover as much as you can about the organization's culture—such as its employee population, its market challenges, its training priorities, and which consulting organizations have worked with the organization in the past.

  ✓ Make sure that your proposal addresses the specific training need outlined in the proposal; do not use the proposal as an introduction to your full complement of services or to sell a more comprehensive training solution.

  ✓ If you include references, make sure they are specific about whom to contact in the organization, his or her title, and when the project was done.

  ✓ Invest in high-quality stationery and binders for your proposal.

  ✓ If you fax or e-mail your proposal, follow up with a hard copy by mail or courier.

  ✓ Beware of presumptuous statements in your cover letter or introduction ("I am sure you want to be the top service provider . . ."). You should, however, refer to information the organization provided, such as a mission statement, and demonstrate how your proposal can support it.

IV
Developing Training Programs

For any training program to be successful, it needs to be engaging, entertaining, and practical. Learners grasp concepts by hearing, seeing, discussing, practicing, and teaching each other. These chapters provide the program designer with the tools to make certain that the learners appreciate the process, retain the information, and are motivated to apply it back on the job.

Lesson Plan Development

"Aim for success, not perfection. Never give up your right to be wrong, because then you will lose the ability to learn new things and move forward with your life."

—DR. DAVID D. BURNS
Psychiatrist and Author of *Feeling Good*

A course without a lesson plan is like a map without a scale. Trainers who follow a clear lesson plan can develop course content that will have a direct impact on the organization's requirements and meet specific skill gaps.

- Both seasoned trainers and line managers are often required to create a lesson plan as a first step in designing a training session, either from scratch or by refining existing training materials.
- A lesson plan is *not:*
  - ✓ A course description for a training catalog
  - ✓ An advertising circular
  - ✓ A facilitator's guide
- A lesson plan is a summary of course outcomes, teaching principles, and methods, that links a training lesson to business planning.
- A lesson plan should include the following components:
  - ✓ Learning objectives
  - ✓ Target audience
  - ✓ Course prerequisites
  - ✓ Key teaching principles
  - ✓ Teaching methodology
  - ✓ Delivery time lines
  - ✓ Materials

Learning Objectives

- Learning objectives should be expressed as outcomes for the participants and make use of action verbs (for example, "At the end of this session, participants will be able to . . .").

- Most courses should have three or four specific outcomes. A single outcome is typically too general to be useful in planning specific training.
- Examples of learning outcomes for a course are:
  - ✓ To recognize selling opportunities
  - ✓ To clarify customer needs
  - ✓ To cut meeting times by 50 percent

Target Audience

- Most courses address specific skill gaps.
- Participants should be identified in terms of a specific level of competence required for certain operating principles or practices (for example, "First-line managers who must carry out performance evaluations consistent with established standards").

Course Prerequisites

- Many courses build on other teaching lessons in either related or preparatory courses (for example, "The feedback principles will build on lessons in the coaching modules"). Previous courses or experience levels should be identified clearly.

Key Teaching Principles

- Teaching principles are the building blocks to stated course outcomes (for example, "The use of open questions as an aid to probing customer concerns").
- Teaching principles identify the context for using the newly acquired skills.

Teaching Methodology

- There are many ways to demonstrate key teaching principles. Examples of teaching methodologies are:
  - ✓ Group exercises

✓ Brainstorming exercises
✓ Team activities
✓ Role plays
✓ Case studies
✓ Simulations

Delivery Time Lines

- Time lines are the allocated time needed to teach the specific principles.
- Time lines are typically organized into modules of related points (for example, Feedback Principles, 2 hours; Introduction to Coaching, 2 hours; Conducting a Performance Interview, 4 hours).

Materials

- Materials include:
  ✓ Participant guides or workbooks
  ✓ Trainer reference materials
  ✓ Videos
  ✓ Overheads

Training Program Design

Training programs can't be developed in a vacuum. They need to be placed in an organizational context and then designed with the specific training needs of the targeted employee(s).

- At the outset of your design efforts:
  ✓ Speak with managers about the organization's operating environment: the political, economic, social, and technological

trends that have an impact on the organization and may give rise to training needs.

✓ Gather information on the organization's short-, medium-, and longer-term objectives to ensure that your training program supports these directions.

✓ Secure your manager's support for the training program, including the funding and time needed to develop and deliver the training.

✓ Check the marketplace to see if a program that might meet your needs and objectives already exists. Ask people who might have attended it what they liked about it and any misgivings that they had as well.

- Determine whether the training will benefit your customers, internal or external. If it will not benefit the customer, do not waste your time and the organization's money.
- Identify when employees need knowledge, skills, or both. If skills are needed, you should incorporate practice into your workshop.
- Plan short sessions rather than one four- or five-day session if the content is highly technical. People retain skills more effectively if you present the training in half-day lessons.
- Learn all you can about your audience:
  ✓ What they need to know
  ✓ What they need to do better
  ✓ Their existing level of performance
  ✓ Their motivation
  ✓ Their literacy
  ✓ If they have any "hot buttons," such as bad experiences in previous training sessions, concerns about downsizing, or low scores in a recent employee satisfaction survey
  ✓ What previous courses they have taken that relate in some way
- In analyzing training needs:
  ✓ Identify the tasks that must be done and the skills required to do them.
  ✓ Check existing job descriptions and vendors' technical manuals for information on these requirements.
  ✓ Conduct an assessment of the skill levels of the employees doing the job.
  ✓ Determine the nature of the performance gap between required and existing skills.

- ✓ Locate existing procedures and check to see if the procedures are still up-to-date.
- ✓ Review any regulations that apply to procedures or conduct.
- ✓ Make sure there is a training need rather than other performance deficiencies, such as a poorly designed job, unrealistic expectations, or an attitude problem.
- Set learning objectives. Document them, and later share them with the trainees. Learning objectives should be:
  - ✓ Stated in clear, simple language, using one objective for each sentence
  - ✓ Listed in a logical order
- Plan your agenda, which should cover:
  - ✓ Welcome and introductions
  - ✓ An icebreaker
  - ✓ Clarification of and buy-in to objectives
  - ✓ Individual training modules
  - ✓ Breaks
  - ✓ Questions and answers
  - ✓ Wrap-up
  - ✓ Evaluation
- Before rolling the training out to everyone:
  - ✓ Test the materials on a pilot group.
  - ✓ Select the pilot group from a cross-section of your potential audience. Be sure to include people who will be forthright and objective in their feedback.
- Time your training so that it is not too early or too late for your objective. If you schedule your session too far in advance of when people need to use the skills, they will forget what you have taught them. Training after they have started will require some unlearning since they may have developed bad habits already.
- To set training priorities:
  - ✓ Determine the impact of the training need on the organization's ability to attain its objectives or comply with legislation.
  - ✓ Identify the impact on the individual employee's ability to succeed at the job.
  - ✓ Assess the cost-to-benefit of the training effort.
- When developing the training content, keep it focused:
  - ✓ Establish clear objectives for the training by completing the sentence: "At the end of this program, the employee(s) will be able to. . . ."

✓ Prepare a high-level outline or blueprint of the program, setting out major content areas or modules, the training objectives for each module, and the expected outcomes of the training.

✓ Select the most suitable combination of instructional techniques: self-study, lecture, one-to-one coaching, video, simulations, case studies, computer-based training, hands-on practice, or interactive learning.

✓ If you use your own design, assemble a small team (including one or two employees from the group to be trained) to validate the training materials before you deliver the program.

✓ Consult subject-matter experts for accuracy.

Methodology—Choosing the Right One

I t is possible to train people using a variety of methods.

- Training can be grouped into two broad categories: self-directed or facilitated. Each has a variety of methods of presenting materials and ideas.
- Self-directed learning gives people the opportunity to take control of their own training. They decide what to learn, how to learn it, when to do it, and where.
- Self-directed learning can be done by:
  ✓ Individual research in books, magazines, and on the Internet
  ✓ Self-paced manuals, tapes, and videos
  ✓ Self-paced computer-based training, accessing information from floppy disks, CD-ROM, the Internet, or the organization's intranet
- Courses that involve using and practicing techniques and processes (budgeting, equipment repair, project management) are better suited to self-directed training media, where the consistency of applying the learning is important.

- Trainer- or facilitator-directed learning gives participants limited control over the content and process of learning. This learning most often takes place in a classroom setting.
- Training courses that focus on learning and practicing skills that involve relationships with others (team, leadership, customer service) are better suited to facilitated learning. In these courses, it is important to discuss reactions and previous experience as part of the learning process.
- Messages in facilitated learning are conducted in any one of the following methods:
  ✓ *Verbal.* This is probably the least effective way. Lecturing as the sole medium of training leads to a retention of approximately 15 percent.
  ✓ *Visual.* People retain more when they see the message. An image is easier to recall than verbal messages. Visual images are conveyed through slides, overheads, and flip charts.
  ✓ *Video.* This method combines visual and verbal messages and is often an effective training tool, particularly if the message is short (under ten minutes) and demonstrations of what is right and wrong closely approximate the real world of the learner.
  ✓ *Role Play.* This method requires the learner to practice a skill, such as conflict resolution or negotiating, after learning some theory. An observer monitors the role play and gives participants feedback on the extent to which they followed a model.
  ✓ *Simulation.* This is the creation of a situation closely akin to the real world, which enables people to be put into situations that produce behavior typically less than desirable. At the end of the exercise, the group debriefs and reviews the observations of participants, observers, and even videos. The learning can be powerful. It can also be threatening and upsetting if feedback is not handled effectively.
  ✓ *Case Study.* After learning points of theory, participants are given a case study to read and analyze. They can be given questions to answer to determine how effectively they applied the theory.
  ✓ *Group Development.* This exercise is facilitated by an experienced person who enables group members to identify and deal with issues that are preventing them from performing at a high level.
- With the availability of multimedia tools and ever-increasing re-

source materials such as books and videos, it is often advisable to conduct lengthy training sessions using a mix of tools as well as facilitated learning.
- Check with other organizations that may have tried certain training tools to get a realistic assessment of their effectiveness.

Role Play: Design and Conduct

Role plays are useful in helping adults apply new concepts and skills and in shifting attitudes. This method of experience-based learning reinforces classroom theory.

Clarity of learning outcomes is essential here. Facilitators need to be able to articulate why they want to use a role play and what they hope to accomplish.

- Benefits of role plays include:
  - ✓ Reinforcing the classroom theory
  - ✓ Allowing adults to practice new skills in a nonthreatening atmosphere
  - ✓ Feedback from peers
  - ✓ Opportunity to experience how others feel
- *Caution*: Adults do not like to feel incompetent or embarrassed. Design role plays with this fact in mind.
- Role plays should be designed so that:
  - ✓ The outcomes are clear.
  - ✓ The steps in the process and time lines are laid out.
  - ✓ People play themselves or a particular role or style.
  - ✓ There is, if possible, an opportunity for participants to practice new behavior as a result of the feedback.
- Role plays work best when:
  - ✓ The scenarios are realistic.
  - ✓ There is adequate time to debrief the process.
  - ✓ The role play is followed by theory to reinforce the learning.

- *Cautions:*
  - ✓ Never skip the debriefing process. Participants need time to come out of their role by talking about how they feel and describing what happened.
  - ✓ If there is not adequate time to debrief the process right after the role play, skip the activity altogether.
- Role plays can occur in pairs, trios, or a group.

Role Plays for Pairs or Trios

- Review the learning outcomes, the steps in the process, and the time available.
  - ✓ Ask people to work in pairs or trios.
  - ✓ Participants choose who will have the major role in demonstrating the skill being learned.
  - ✓ Designate a third person to act as an observer.
  - ✓ Provide observation sheets and guidelines for the observer.
  - ✓ Provide feedback sheets to assist the observer in giving feedback.
  - ✓ Allow preparation time if needed to study the role or relevant information.
  - ✓ The facilitator's role is to observe the groups but not intervene unless participants are off-track or step out of role.
  - ✓ Call time at the end of the first role play.
  - ✓ Allow time for debriefing—feedback from either the receiver or the observer.
  - ✓ Have participants switch roles.
  - ✓ Each member of the pair or trio should have the opportunity to be the giver or initiator.
  - ✓ Repeat this process.
  - ✓ When the pairs or trios have completed the role play, allow for large-group discussion of what people learned.

Role Plays in Groups

- Within a group setting, each individual plays an assigned role in accomplishing a particular task. This type of role play can be used to demonstrate:

- ✓ Teamwork
- ✓ Meetings
- ✓ Leadership styles
- ✓ Conflict resolution
- When particular roles are assigned to individuals:
  - ✓ Hand out copies of each of the roles to each person.
  - ✓ Emphasize that the details supplied for each role are confidential.
  - ✓ Allow time for preparation for the role play.
  - ✓ Explain that team members cannot reveal to other members their particular role until the role is over.
- Steps for group role plays:
  - ✓ Review the learning outcomes, the steps in the process, and the time available.
  - ✓ Allow preparation time.
  - ✓ The facilitator's role is to observe the group's process but not to intervene unless people have misunderstood the instructions or are out of role.
  - ✓ Call time at the end.
  - ✓ Facilitate the debriefing of the process:
    - How do people feel after the role play?
    - What happened?
    - Why did that happen?
    - How might that have been handled differently?
    - Who had control of the discussion?
    - Did anyone feel left out?
  - ✓ Add some of your own observations and ask for explanations and comments from the group.
  - ✓ Encourage everyone to speak.
  - ✓ Allow participants to explain the role they were playing.
  - ✓ Reinforce the learning points with relevant theory.

Case Studies

A case study is a description of a realistic work situation that high-lights a problem. The problem can be resolved in a variety of ways, using principles and theory given earlier to the trainee.

- Case studies are typically documented in writing, but can be in video format, too.
- Analysis and problem solving can be done individually, in groups, or combined (individually, then comparing answers in groups).
- A good case study does the following:
  ✓ Covers one area of theory
  ✓ Is intellectually challenging
  ✓ Is realistic
  ✓ Is customized to suit the audience in terms of its description of the organization, products, customers, culture, and other factors
  ✓ Provides adequate time to enable detailed analysis and discussion
- The logical order of using case studies is as follows:
  ✓ Hand out the case study.
  ✓ Review the steps you will be taking and the time allowance. Check for understanding from the participants.
  ✓ Allow time for people to read the material.
  ✓ Allow people to read the questions individually and write down their answers. This will challenge everyone to think before the group discussion.
  ✓ Set up groups to analyze the case. This can be done by randomly counting off people and having everyone with the same number work together. Or, try to mix people up so that the greatest variety of personalities and backgrounds are together. (Homogeneous groups learn less and finish quickly.)
  ✓ Appoint a facilitator in each group of four to eight people. Otherwise, the group might rely on the most knowledgeable person for the answers, finish quickly, and learn very little.
  ✓ Debrief the exercise. Have a spokesperson from each group report the group's answer to each question. So as not to duplicate discussion, ask other groups if they have a different answer or

additional issues to bring up. Then repeat the process for the next question, and so on, until completion.

✓ Summarize the discussion, highlight key issues, and match theory and practice.

Training Materials

M aterials are important during and after training. Here are some ideas as to how to make them as effective as possible.

- Bear in mind that the audience will include people who learn best in one of three ways: visual, auditory, and kinesthetic. Your presentation should include all three modalities for maximum impact.
- Decide on the best medium for the visual part of the presentation. The most commonly used media are slides or overheads for a formal presentation or flip charts for an informal presentation. People require about 40 percent less time to grasp a concept with visual aids than with verbal instruction alone.
- If you use slides or overheads:
  ✓ Keep them short and to the point.
  ✓ Use one idea per transparency or slide.
  ✓ Add pictures where possible.
  ✓ Make sure that letters are large, bold, and legible.
- Develop materials to suit the audience. For example, materials for people with poor literacy should have more pictures and diagrams.
- Materials will work better if they:
  ✓ Contain one idea per page
  ✓ Are written in simple language
  ✓ Have lots of space to make notes
  ✓ Are interactive, with spaces for people to write answers, do quizzes, and complete checklists
- You have two choices with regard to materials:
  1. Develop your own
  2. Buy a ready-made program

Ready-Made Programs

- Consider buying a packaged program if development costs are high. Avoid packages that:
  - ✓ Will date quickly (high-tech subjects are particularly vulnerable)
  - ✓ Cannot be customized
  - ✓ Have audiovisuals from a different industry
  - ✓ Are aimed at a different audience level
  - ✓ Are made in a foreign country
- An ideal packaged program:
  - ✓ Can be tried before you commit
  - ✓ Is recommended by others in your industry
  - ✓ Lends itself to easy updating
  - ✓ Can be duplicated without breaking any copyright

Developing Your Own Materials

- Ensure that your materials include:
  - ✓ A title page
  - ✓ A letter of endorsement from a sponsor, such as the president
  - ✓ A table of contents
  - ✓ Instructions on how to use the manual
  - ✓ The body content
  - ✓ Appropriate appendixes
- In assembling the content for the manual, refer to the following:
  - ✓ Existing materials
  - ✓ Documents from the work area that the training is being designed for
  - ✓ Human resources professionals who may shed light on any corporate policies that have a bearing on your subject matter
  - ✓ Legal counsel, should the topic be subject to legislation at the local or national level
- The language in your workbook should:
  - ✓ Talk to, never down to, participants
  - ✓ Be written in a style that is easy to read and conversational in tone
  - ✓ Make use of clear, short, and familiar words
  - ✓ Not include words that do not add to the meaning of any sentence

✓ Be free of jargon

✓ Have short sentences that contain one thought only

✓ Use point form wherever possible

✓ Emphasize key ideas or words by making them bold, italicized, or underlined

✓ Avoid sexist language or the use of only male pronouns

✓ Contain lots of white space for trainees to make notes

✓ Be interspersed with exercises that will allow trainees to document their own ideas or answer a quiz

✓ Contain numerous diagrams, pictures, and charts

✓ Contain chapters for each new topic, clearly designated with a chapter-opening page.

Simulations

A simulation is a lifelike enactment, in a classroom-type setting, of the realities of the job. It tests people's ability to apply learning principles.

- Simulations can be used in the following two situations:
  1. Training
  2. As part of assessing prospective employees
- In training, simulations encourage participants to demonstrate their use of newly acquired skills.
- Assessment centers have become increasingly popular, particularly in organizations that are hiring a number of people simultaneously. Simulations enable trained observers to see how people:
  ✓ Respond under pressure
  ✓ Work in a team environment
  ✓ Manage priorities
- Adults enjoy simulations because it gives them a chance to:
  ✓ Practice a skill
  ✓ Obtain positive feedback
  ✓ Build the confidence to use the skill
  ✓ Confirm that they understand the theory being taught

- Simulations can take the form of the following formats:
  - ✓ Role plays
  - ✓ Games
  - ✓ Dramatizations of real situations
- The advantages of a simulation include:
  - ✓ Practice in a nonthreatening environment
  - ✓ Allowing mistakes off rather than on the job
- Simulations work best when the following principles are followed:
  - ✓ The simulation is done right after a key teaching lesson.
  - ✓ The exercise is realistic; there is no need to stretch the imagination to discover how it might apply in the workplace.
  - ✓ The time allowed does not go beyond what is needed to learn the key principles.
  - ✓ Sufficient time is available to debrief and provide feedback to participants. The debriefing should cover what was done well and what might have been done differently.
  - ✓ The exercise's complexity is geared to the skill levels of the participants.
  - ✓ The exercise has clearly defined objectives.
- Key design features of successful simulations include:
  - ✓ Having the feeling of being a real situation that has either just happened or is about to happen.
  - ✓ Allowing the participants to exceed a satisfactory outcome. This will increase confidence.
  - ✓ Detailed instructions, both oral and written.
  - ✓ A flexible design that allows people to customize the details to make them fit better with their world.
  - ✓ The possibility of failure, to allow for learning as a result of the simulation.
  - ✓ Sufficient time for people to regroup and correct their mistakes.
  - ✓ Sufficient time to make it real, but not too long that it drags and leads to boredom.
  - ✓ Checklists that allow participants to record their observations about the use and frequency of the newly acquired skill.

Pilot Programs

A pilot program is a test run for a major training program that allows trainers and developers to make adjustments based on realistic feedback from participants, developers, and managers.

- As a general rule, pilot programs should be considered for any program that will entail at least 1,000 trainee hours (for example, 200 participants for a five-day course.) The course may be either classroom or technology based. This typically applies to:
  - ✓ Training large groups that must receive a consistent message and support for key skills
  - ✓ Training that supports the introduction or upgrade of expensive equipment
  - ✓ Training that will/must be delivered at different levels and in different locations
  - ✓ Training that will be conducted over a period longer than a year
- The team for evaluating and adjusting a pilot should consist of representatives from:
  - ✓ The client group (the *client* is the owner of the business process; for example, customer service: sales dept., coaching skills: human resources)
  - ✓ Design and development team (these may be internal or external parties)
  - ✓ Skilled facilitators and trainers who will not be delivering the course (these are more likely to see the "bigger picture" than designated facilitators)
  - ✓ Representative trainees from the target training population
- Designate a member of the team to:
  - ✓ Set parameters—what costs and time commitments are realistic for making changes now; what adjustments might occur after multiple presentations.
  - ✓ Determine what the priority decisions are—that is, content, course length, and so forth.
  - ✓ Beyond overall impressions, assign specific tasks to each evaluation team member, for example, observing participant energy

levels; observing whether exercises can be conducted in the suggest time frames.

✓ Set a deadline for gathering observations and making changes.

✓ Design a simple tool for written observations (rather than collecting only verbal impressions). The tool should emphasize the intended outcome of the course (one or two key learning objectives) as the basis for observations.

- The elements of the course that will be evaluated include:
  ✓ Pre- and post-course assignments
  ✓ Logical sequencing of messages and materials
  ✓ Appropriate course length
  ✓ Meaningful skill outcomes for practice exercises
  ✓ Balance of lecturing and participation
  ✓ Technical reliability of any training technology
  ✓ Clarity of learning outcomes
  ✓ Usefulness of the course evaluation questionnaire
  ✓ Participant and customer satisfaction

- The following questions should be reviewed after a pilot presentation:
  ✓ Is the room size and set-up important to the learning?
  ✓ Is the subject matter likely to change over time, and if so, how will the course be adapted?
  ✓ If training technology is involved, is there adequate technical support at all training locations?
  ✓ Does the course rely on trainers who are specifically trained for the launch? Can other trainers—at other locations—be brought up to speed?

- Here are some cautions about conducting a pilot program:
  ✓ Do not have more than three observers in the room; large teams of observers can dominate and distract the actual participants.
  ✓ Beware of the tendency to observe only what is wrong, rather than what is working.
  ✓ Do not choose a select group of participants or high performers for a pilot; this will not give you a realistic picture of the typical trainee population.
  ✓ Do not rely solely on post-course evaluations; follow up with trainees two or three weeks after the course is completed.

V
Delivery Options

M odern technology allows us to train people in the four corners of the globe simultaneously. Part V examines the increasing number of options available and reviews the merits of each.

Technology: Choosing High-Tech or Low-Tech

Decisions about the appropriate medium for a training course begin with the client who is sponsoring the training initiative. Choosing the best medium begins with an understanding of the key objectives for the program.

- The following questions are helpful when meeting with in-house clients to set objectives:
  - ✓ How was the training need identified?
  - ✓ How will a program's success be measured?
  - ✓ Is the training need a business need, a turnover requirement, or a personal-development need?
  - ✓ Should the current in-house program be updated to reflect new corporate policies or procedures?
  - ✓ Does every employee in the target group need the training?
  - ✓ Will the program be repeated year after year for new audiences?
  The answers to these questions will give an overall scope to the program, in terms of size, success measures, target population, and continuing availability.
- The emergence of sophisticated multimedia training tools has been heralded as a cost-effective way to manage learning for large populations. This has also sparked debate about the effectiveness of classroom training versus individual learning, together with the costs and benefits of each.
- There are four training medium choices:
  1. Classroom training
  2. Multimedia training for group presentations
  3. Self-directed tools (e-learning)
  4. Blended learning that combines all or some of the above
- Factors that influence the appropriate choice are:
  - ✓ Current technology proficiency and confidence level of participants
  - ✓ Importance of practice and immediate feedback to the intended learning outcome

✓ Development deadline and budget
✓ Numbers of employees in the target population
✓ Geographical distribution of target population
✓ Measurement tools to assess learning outcomes
- These elements will help you to create a situation analysis for assessing the advantages and disadvantages for a *high-tech* or *low-tech* environment.

Multimedia (High-Tech)

Advantages	Disadvantages
• reduced demand on trainers	• assumes computer literacy
• provides remote site delivery	• no immediate response to difficult questions
• employees learn at their own paces	• expensive to develop and install
• consistent delivery	• no chance to practice new skills for immediate feedback
• modules can be used for follow-up and refresher trainings	• no interaction with other learners
• reduces travel and facilities costs	• cannot be easily updated

Classroom Training (Low-Tech)

Advantages	Disadvantages
• more participative and energizing	• difficult to schedule employees
• provides hands-on practice	• expensive scheduling and administrative time
• trainer can monitor impact	• requires guaranteed number of participants

- can be adapted to specific skill levels
- travel costs for both partici- pants and facilitators
- opportunity to learn from others

- The following important considerations go beyond cost and avail- ability:
  ✓ Many teleworkers prefer training where they can interact with others.
  ✓ Trainees should only be learning one key skill in a course, so ensure that they are not learning to cope with the technology as well.
  ✓ The mix of trainees: Are they all operating at the same skill level before the training? If not, independent learning may be advis- able.
- More and more programs are combining elements of classroom learning with online availability for complex lessons and self-paced follow-up, which combines the advantages of both high-tech and low-tech solutions.

E-Learning

E lectronic or e-learning can be defined as any type of learning that is enhanced, either partially or fully, by some electronic form of communication. Electronically delivered learning will become in- creasingly important as tools become easier and less expensive, and technologies become available to people around the world. A great deal of confusion exists around e-learning, so here is an overview of the topic looking at it from both the training manager's and the learn- er's perspective.

- There are many forms of e-learning. The most common are:
  ✓ In-house computer training
  ✓ Web-based training

- In-house learning refers to skills development on a single subject, typically contained on a CD-ROM. The CD will allow the learner to conduct his or her own training in a self-paced process that could be done either individually or in a classroom. Working with an instructor enables the less-secure learner to ask for help in the event of technical problems.
- The two types of available Web-based training are:
  ✓ Asynchronous training
  ✓ Synchronous training

Asynchronous training is learning that allows trainees to log in to a Web site and choose from a menu of topics so that they can learn on their own. Synchronous training, on the other hand, is training that is offered on the Web that is done in a virtual classroom and is led by a facilitator. The students are located remotely, using their computers, to follow a lesson and interact as the need may arise.

Web-based training will become increasingly popular because it has several advantages, including:

- *Reduction of Costs.* The dollars associated with off-premise training can be considerable. The costs of travel, accommodation, and time away from work often exceed the cost of the actual training. This is a significant consideration for people outside of metropolitan areas.
- *Ability to Include a Mobile Workforce.* Increasing numbers of people are operating in a virtual environment, with many working from home offices and hotel rooms around the globe. Having them all receive the same training, with the same message, can be important.
- *Flexibility.* Asynchronous training allows learners to take a module anytime they have the time and inclination. Synchronous training also allows for some flexibility as modules are typically scheduled in advance, taking typically ninety minutes from a person's work week instead of an entire day or days.
- Web-based synchronous training has several advantages for the participants, because they can:
  ✓ Do projects together, such as construct a spreadsheet or map a process—both of which have real-world value
  ✓ Find examples of a concept on the Web at the same time that they are monitoring the program

✓ Have access to virtually every library and book that exists
✓ Meet new peer groups around the world, with whom they can share wisdom
✓ Develop networks that are likely to continue long after the formal sessions have been completed

- Web-based training is particularly suited to people who share the following characteristics:
  ✓ Are mobile
  ✓ Time pressured
  ✓ Self-directed and determined to complete their program
  ✓ Comfortable with technology
  ✓ Have access to a reliable ISP provider (taken for granted in most Western countries)
- Evaluating a Web-based program can be challenging. Delivery platforms should be compared for their ease of use, reliability, and support.
- A good asynchronous program (and module) should be designed so that:
  ✓ The technology can be demonstrated for first-time users.
  ✓ The vendor has 24/7 technical assistance available on an 800 number.
  ✓ Each module:
    - Has clearly defined objectives and an agenda
    - Is short and to the point
    - Allows the user to see and hear the text as well as videos of behaviors that may be illustrated in soft-skill training
    - Should not exceed fifteen minutes in length before it stops to obtain feedback from the participant in the form of a quiz
  ✓ Programs are available in multiple languages to suit the learner's needs.
  ✓ The moderator can:
    - Move forward or back using PowerPoint slides
    - Track who has logged in
    - Mute some or all of the lines
    - "Lock" or "unlock" the workshop at any time
    - Have instant access to technical support
    - Track participative behavior such as the time logged in and out and time when the participant might have wandered away from the computer
  ✓ Modules should be staggered so that people can fit them into a

busy work schedule. Experience suggests that each module should not exceed ninety minutes in length nor have more than twenty people in the virtual classroom. Less is better.

✓ It can be recorded and accessed via the Web by students who might have missed the session.

• Web-based synchronous training programs are new to the vast majority of learners and training managers. For the trainer, there are many advantages, such as:

✓ Being able to network with people around the world.

✓ Access to trainees who would never have this opportunity.

✓ The ability to work at home in your pajamas!

✓ No requirement for you to be in a classroom; you can teach from wherever you happen to be: in your office, at home, or on the road.

• Evaluation of Web-based synchronous training is difficult; however, the most effective of these programs provide:

✓ Full-duplex sound technology that allows voice and data to flow both ways *simultaneously*. Previous generations would only allow for transfers of voice and data to be one at a time, thereby blocking one source that may be transmitting inadvertently.

✓ Secure access to its own URL with password protection.

✓ The use of the PC to deliver visual signals but separates the audio, which can be delivered as Voice over Internet Protocol (VoIP) or via the telephone.

✓ Adequate staffing to ensure success, including:

  • A facilitator who has the ability to communicate clearly and adjust his/her voice to advantage

  • A technical "copilot" who is available to ensure that the service is being provided with no hitches

✓ Access via an international toll-free number.

• Features of excellent Web-based software include:

✓ An ability to move back and forward in the materials

✓ Instant access to help via two media: a help button on the screen and a help desk

✓ Information about the instructor

✓ An ability to interact with the instructor and other participants

✓ An ability to pause the materials (slides)

✓ An ability to see all the materials (slides)

✓ Reference links, such as URLs

✓ An ability to bookmark materials, if called away

✓ An ability to see the notes on each slide
✓ A quiz to check for understanding
- There are drawbacks to Web-based programs, which include:
  ✓ Lack of consistent adequate technology internationally. While the technology may be global, the access is dependent on local availability of reliable telephone services—something people take for granted in Western countries.
  ✓ A perceived lack of social contact. Although people can interact with each other, soft-skills training is undoubtedly better face-to-face.
  ✓ Difficulty in doing some types of experiential exercises, such as group work.
  ✓ Catering primarily to auditory and visual learners and less to kinesthetic learners.
  ✓ Unforeseen technical hitches and other irritants may include:
    - Participants putting their telephones on hold and having the rest of the group subjected to music that kicks in
    - Participants' not having immediate access because the computer they are using has temporarily lost access to the Internet because the local provider is "down"
    - A local computer the participant is using has an older version of the Web browser and is unable to log in
    - A telephone echo that makes some feel like they talking to people on another planet
  ✓ Difficulties with group dynamics that are multiplied when the facilitator is not able to see what is happening and has to rely on participants speaking up; this includes the following:
    - People not listening to each other and then asking questions that have been dealt with
    - One or two people dominating the conversations
    - Participants not using features such as "raising hands" and sending text questions, thereby allowing the moderator to exercise control over the group
    - One or two participants speaking continuously when not asked or required, thereby interrupting the flow of information for the other participants
    - Participants refusing to use the software features such as "raising hands," allowing the moderator to invite comments at appropriate times

- Deciding on whether to create an organization's own Web-based training program will be influenced by factors such as:
  ✓ The size of the organization
  ✓ Its geographical spread
  ✓ Available resources
  ✓ The type of people it wishes to train (technical abilities)
  ✓ Sophistication of the designers and access to appropriate technology
  ✓ Availability of a suitable vendor with which it can partner

Videoconferencing

"Words mean more than what is set down on paper. It takes the human voice to infuse them with shades of deeper meaning."

—MAYA ANGELOU
Poet, Educator, Author, and Activist

Videoconferencing is the process whereby people all around the world can gather at prearranged facilities and participate in training. This format is most frequently used to bring the biggest audience at reasonable cost to listen to popular speakers who typically command fees running into tens of thousands of dollars. This format is also being used by business schools that are increasingly encroaching into the territories of other schools with the objective of adding to their student populations and revenues.

- Videoconferencing works best when:
  ✓ The system is backed by reliable technology that guarantees 100 percent uptime.
  ✓ Images are available on a big screen allowing everyone in the audience to see the speaker clearly.
  ✓ The speaker can cut to a split screen from time to time so that the audience can see complementary slides.

✓ Time is provided for local discussion.

✓ The information is interesting but not too complex. The presenter is generally unable to know whether a point is understood or not.

✓ There are sufficient short breaks to allow people to clear their heads, stretch, and prepare for more information download.

✓ Participants are not packed into halls with theater-style seating, but are given the opportunity to have a workbench to put materials on, including laptops.

- The success of the training greatly depends on having an excellent presenter. Ideally, he or she should:

  ✓ Be respected in his or her field

  ✓ Have an excellent presence

  ✓ Be able to ad-lib without the use of notes

  ✓ Have a strong, commanding voice

  ✓ Be animated and engaging

- Videoconferencing may not be the most effective tool to promote learning retention as the process rarely allows for practice of the skills. Therefore, it is a good medium for theory only but needs to be supplemented by local group work that encourages discussion and practice, if appropriate. A good program will use only part of the time for presentation, with the balance of the time being given for small group discussion.

- If the audience is not too widely dispersed and the number of students not too large, it may be possible to provide some interaction between the audience and the presenter. This can be done by providing microphones interspersed around the room for questions from the audience or to enable small-group spokespersons to present key ideas.

Self-Directed Learning

> *"We can only have citizens who can live constructively in the kaleidoscopically changing world . . . if we are willing for them to become self-starting, self-initiating learners."*
>
> —CARL ROGERS
> Psychologist and Author of *Freedom to Learn*

Many individuals are capable and willing to take responsibility for their own learning. These people can create and monitor their own progress toward learning goals using fewer resources.

- Self-directed learners are more willing to:
    - ✓ Take the initiative to learn
    - ✓ Diagnose their own needs
    - ✓ Set learning goals
    - ✓ Find the resources
    - ✓ Pick the method of learning that most appeals to them
    - ✓ Implement the learning
    - ✓ Evaluate the outcome
- Knowledge and skills can be acquired independently in a number of ways:
    - ✓ Books
    - ✓ Self-study programs on tape (audio disk)
    - ✓ Videos
    - ✓ Self-paced textbooks
    - ✓ Computer-based training
    - ✓ Interactive video
    - ✓ Internet-accessed materials
    - ✓ Mentors
    - ✓ Coworkers
    - ✓ Magazine and journal articles
    - ✓ Observation
    - ✓ On-site courses
    - ✓ Workshops and seminars
- The advantages of self-directed learning are:

✓ The learner has control over pace.
✓ Ownership is high.
✓ Costs are low.
✓ The learner can customize the content.
✓ Training can take place during slow periods of the day.
- Some disadvantages of self-directed learning are:
  ✓ Most programs contain generic materials, parts of which may be unhelpful for the learner.
  ✓ Written materials usually can be used only once and cannot be duplicated without breaking copyright laws.
  ✓ It is difficult to learn managerial skills by any method other than experiential. An understanding of materials may not lead to effective application.
  ✓ The rate of dropout of self-directed programs is higher than that facilitated by a trained instructor.
- Strategies to evaluate packaged programs include:
  ✓ Comparing the documented objective against your own.
  ✓ Checking with others who have used the materials. (Be cautious of this information. Consultants are unlikely to supply the names of unhappy customers.)
  ✓ Checking with your own network of trainers.
  ✓ An estimation of the shelf life of the materials. The longer you can use them without a major update, the more cost-effective they become. Technical subjects date a lot quicker than managerial topics.
  ✓ Calculating and comparing the cost per trainee for each program.
- The following guidelines are important when using self-directed learning programs:
  ✓ Ensure that materials, such as workbooks and computers, are always available.
  ✓ Make coaches available for those who need encouragement, guidance, and redirection if they hit a roadblock.
  ✓ Provide opportunities for people to check their knowledge through self-scoring systems or tests that can be checked by an expert.
  ✓ Check that the majority of people reach their objective.
  ✓ If course-learning objectives are not being met by most people, investigate the cause.

✓ If dropout rates begin to rise, find out the reason and fix the problem.

✓ Regularly update materials to ensure that they are easy to follow and error-free.

✓ Pilot-test new programs to remove bugs.

- Self-directed learning is enhanced if the learner commits to a written plan. It will "force" participants to:

  ✓ Develop clear learning objectives

  ✓ Identify actions that will lead to the achievement of those objectives

  ✓ Set completion dates

  ✓ Decide how they will know in measurable terms when they are finished

An example of a format for this plan can be found in Exhibit 6.

Exhibit 6. Self-directed learning plan.

My Learning Objectives	The Steps I Intend to Take	Target Date	Evaluation Method

Computer-Based Training

"I do not fear computers. I fear the lack of them."

—ISAAC ASIMOV
Futurist and Author

C omputers are becoming a dominant tool for training, as well as the predominant tool for communicating. In fact, this medium is growing faster than other forms of training delivery. Here is an overview on the use of CD-ROMs and interactive videodisks.

- Computer-based training (CBT) refers to learning that is conducted through the medium of a computer. The applications of this mode of instruction are growing daily in terms of quantity and quality. While earlier versions of CBT focused on the individual learning on his or her own, the advent of the Web has made distance education, with a live moderator, accessible to people around the world. The primary methods of computer-based training include:
  ✓ Interactive videodisk instruction
  ✓ CD-ROM
  ✓ Web-based distance online learning
  ✓ Web-based training on demand
- CBT is a fascinating and exciting medium for training, but it is by no means immune to problems of poor design.
- As more people become exposed to animation, virtual reality, and the sophistication of video games, it has become increasingly difficult to design videodisk and CD-ROMs that will challenge, stimulate, and hold the attention of learners for any reasonable time, let alone teach them.
- Experience shows that CBT, like other forms of training, needs to be:
  ✓ Focused on a single topic
  ✓ Customized for a particular organization or industry
  ✓ Integrated into other forms of learning that will reinforce and lend variety to the learning experience
- CBT can never take the place of human interaction. It is unrealistic to consider CBT as the ultimate and only form of training.

- CBT is most effective when it is designed to work like the human brain, an undisciplined organ that likes to flow from one idea to another. Therefore, CBT that provides only for multiple-choice responses or enables a person to move from one screen to the next in a predesigned sequence will be far less effective than a process that:
  - ✓ Allows the learner to move to topics of his or her choice in a random fashion
  - ✓ Provides feedback on the learner's effectiveness, particularly when the person has made a mistake
  - ✓ Enables the learner to use a variety of tools to navigate through the learning process
- CBT that relies on sound, animation, and color to maintain learners' attention is much less effective than a technology that allows for an interactive response through video clips or responsive animation.

VI
Conducting Training

Preparation for Training

"Spectacular achievement is always preceded by spectacular preparation."

—ROBERT H. SCHULLER
Televangelist

Proper preparation for training will allow you to present information in a relaxed, effective, and professional manner. The following list will help you to avoid some common pitfalls.

- Book meeting rooms early, advise attendees of the location, and provide maps to it if necessary.
- Confirm the number of attendees.
- Assemble your materials and supporting documentation.
- Confirm your meeting room reservation and ensure that refreshments have been ordered.
- If the presentation is complex, have a package of information prepared for each participant. Distribute these packages in advance for everyone to review prior to the session.
- Do a dry run to test the materials and your self-confidence. Imagine the audience in front of you. Gauge their reaction. Consider videotaping your practice session so that you can refine it as may be appropriate.
- Review your objectives to make sure they are in line with what you intend to deliver. Better still, make sure that what you intend to deliver is directly related to the objectives.
- Assemble a backup emergency kit of markers, masking tape, name cards, pencils, pens, and spare bulbs for equipment.
- Meet with some attendees beforehand to gauge their enthusiasm for the upcoming presentation or their concerns. If you detect any resistance, give them an opportunity to vent by:
  - ✓ Listening
  - ✓ Showing empathy
  - ✓ Offering to address their concern if at all possible
- Learn as much as you can about the training audience: their skill levels, demographics, and prior training experiences.

- Test-drive the overhead projector, VCR, and room lighting.
- Review the evaluations from other groups to whom you've given the course. Determine which topics generated the least interest or most confusion, and analyze why.
- Talk with the manager or managers of the participants to find out as much as you can about their learning styles, communication styles, and general enthusiasm about training.
- Get a sense of other organization issues that may be playing on the trainees' minds: downsizing, new performance measures, upcoming management changes, and so forth.
- Develop a workplace profile of the group. Is there some natural tension among participants already (for example, managers attending along with their direct reports? union and nonunion employees in the group? salaried and hourly employees?)
- Conduct an informal telephone survey with some participants to understand their expectations and previous training experiences, good and bad.
- Call someone who has trained the group before. What are this person's observations?
- Develop a short quiz for trainees to complete (anonymously) before training. Focus on their expectations and their experience in the subject matter.
- Arrive at the session as early as possible to mingle with the group, and get a sense about their enthusiasm for the subject matter.

Icebreakers

"The only joy in the world is to begin."

—CESARE PAVESE
Novelist

The use of icebreakers is a great way to get a session off and running with everyone more comfortable and receptive to the process. They help people relax and loose inhibitions that might prevent them from participating though questions, discussions, and experiential exercises. This chapter contains some ideas to do it right.

Not all icebreakers work. Some might bomb and cast a shadow on the rest of your training day. To avoid an exercise that increases tension and apprehension, consider the following:

- Don't do anything that would cause you discomfort or annoyance if *you* were a participant.
- Adjust the length of the icebreaker to suit the length of the session. A more extensive icebreaker would work for a workshop that lasts two to five days, whereas a quick exercise (of two to five minutes) would be appropriate for a session of one day or less.
- Know your audience. Not all adults are ready to do something a little silly early on in the workshop. Generally, the more senior that people are, the less they might want to do anything that puts them at risk of looking foolish. People's dress might give you a clue as to how much participants will engage in risky activities early on in the session. The rule is to play it more conservatively with people in business suits, and expect people who are casually dressed to stretch.
- People who know each other may find some exercises redundant. A mixed audience of people from different organizations would benefit more from getting to know more about each other.
- In-house workshops require fewer risky icebreakers than those taking place at a resort.
- Learning that deals with "soft" subjects such as conflict and communications benefits more from an icebreaker than one that focuses on learning computer software.
- Participants who work with people—as opposed to equipment or technology—might enjoy a more unusual exercise than participants with limited personal contact in their jobs.
- Examples of some low-risk icebreakers include:
  - ✓ Having people introduce themselves
  - ✓ Creating two-person teams and asking the partners to introduce the other by name, job, learning objectives, and something unusual about the person
  - ✓ Having people describe their most unusual training experience
  - ✓ Adding up the total years of business experience of all the participants, a great way to point out the opportunity to learn from each other

- More adventurous and time-consuming icebreakers include:
  - ✓ A team simulation that shows the value of working together.
  - ✓ A scavenger hunt in which people are given a list of unusual statements about people. They then need to approach most people in the room to match the statement—for example, "has seven kids and eight cats"—with the person. To encourage mixing, a prize can be awarded to the first person to complete the exercise.

Overcoming Nervousness

"Confronting your fears and allowing yourself the right to be human can, paradoxically, make you a far happier and more productive person."

—DR. DAVID D. BURNS
Medical Doctor and Philosopher

Some people are not comfortable talking in front of others, and many a speech has been destroyed by the resulting anxiety. Here are some techniques to help you reduce your butterflies. Remember: Everyone has some apprehensions before training. Some tension produces performance-enhancing adrenaline.

One Day Before Training

- Prepare, prepare, prepare. There are many things trainees will forgive; inadequate preparation is not one of them.
- Anticipate potential reactions or concerns and questions trainees will have.
- Learn as much as you can about the potential audience: their average skill level, demographics, and prior training experiences.
- Ask some of the trainees what you can do to make the session successful.

- Ask the client what he or she expects the training experience to achieve.
- Prepare index cards with key introductory information.

One Hour Before Training

- Check out the training room—its heating, seating, equipment, and lights.
- Test-drive the overhead projector, VCR, and any other equipment you will use.
- Walk around the room to get a sense of the trainees' perspective.
- Lay out your overheads in order, and line up marking pens and masking tape.
- Talk to everyone you run into, about anything. Don't make your introduction your first verbal foray of the day.
- Stop preparing. Last-minute reviews only heighten your sense of doom.
- Spend a few minutes alone before the presentation to collect your thoughts and focus your energy.
- Eliminate possible distractions on your person—for instance, bracelets that clang and loose change jiggling in your pocket.

Immediately Before the Session

- Shake hands with participants as they enter the room to reinforce the one-on-one relationship.
- Remind yourself that trainees are coming to learn, not to be impressed by your talent.
- Chat briefly with as many people as you can.
- Remind yourself that the group really does want you to succeed (have a little faith in human nature).
- Before you start, take a few deep breaths to regulate your breathing.

During the Introduction

- If you have a small audience, begin your presentation casually with a two-way discussion of something topical. This will reduce tension and allow you to ease into the training.

- Be sincere. Don't overdo the enthusiasm, which can ring false.
- Make individual eye contact with as many people as possible at the start.
- Ignore advice that says you should always start with a joke. A flat joke is worse than a flat introduction.
- Do use humor if you feel comfortable doing so. If you do, make sure that it is relevant, and preferably something personal.
- Use cue cards instead of a written script. You will speak normally (with eye contact), and keep in touch with your audience.
- Be yourself. Emulating someone else will make you feel awkward, and the audience will react with skepticism.
- Maintain eye contact with a friendly face in the audience—someone who smiles or nods at you when you make a point. This positive feedback will increase your confidence and let you know how you are doing. Similarly, avoid eye contact with someone who is looking unhappy.
- Don't fiddle with a pointer, pen, change in your pocket, or anything else that may be handy. You will distract the audience.
- Consider sitting down if you can be seen by all the participants; this gives a sense of working together.
- Recognize that people come to training sessions with varying degrees of enthusiasm.
- If all else fails, acknowledge your nervousness briefly; point out that it is a mark of respect for your audience.
- Remember that it is mathematically impossible for one person to be smarter than the combined experience and resources of the group. You are there to leverage learning, not to outdo participants' skills and aptitudes.

Impact in the Classroom

Training isn't theater, but adding a little drama can increase the audience's attention during the session and aid retention afterward. The following suggestions will add impact to sessions:

- Invite senior executives to drop by unannounced for informal question-and-answer sessions.
- Hand out personalized letters from the organization's president to all participants at the beginning of the session, outlining his or her expectations for the course and for active participation.
- Videotape a breakout session, and play it later in the course. Have participants comment on learning styles and teamwork after watching the tape.
- Have participants nominate "winners" at the end of sessions—for example, "best contributor," "most helpful," "best team player," or "best sense of humor." Give out business books or other prizes.
- During customer service courses, have participants prepare a report card about the quality of service received during meals throughout the course. Use specific observations to emphasize key teaching lessons.
- Invite previous participants to the classroom to discuss how they applied specific principles they learned from the course.
- During lengthy courses, let participants spend an afternoon in a local library to compile a bibliography of books related to the course content.
- At the end of a course, have participants develop a learning contract with a buddy for follow-up after the course.
- At the end of the course, have one group develop a true-or-false quiz about the teaching principles for the rest of the group to answer.
- At the end of the course, do a composite portrait of all the best attitudes and actions of participants that contributed to the success of the course. Send the summary out to everyone afterward.
- Involve the group in competitive intelligence exercises. Have group members interview family and friends to understand how other organizations cope with issues that are highlighted during training.
- Do some open-book exercises. Have business articles and contemporary management books on hand, so that participants can do some hands-on research about business issues and practices.
- Using games such as *Scrabble* or *Pictionary*, let participants compete as teams to demonstrate and reinforce the dynamics of group decision making.
- Use self-assessment exercises as often as possible. Few people can resist the impulse to discover more about themselves.
- Use current recruitment advertisements to demonstrate the kinds

of characteristics and qualifications that management and leadership positions require. Relate this information to your own organization.

- Use someone from your organization's advertising department to lead the group in a brainstorming session and to talk about creative brainstorming techniques.
- To focus a discussion, use examples of obvious bloopers that other organizations have made. Let participants contribute examples from their own experiences.
- Invite selected customers to talk about their expectations for the organization.
- Invite an industry expert to discuss contemporary issues over lunch.
- Allow five minutes for participants to sit with someone whom they don't know well and learn about that person's role and background.
- Arrange for a short tour of a facility or department close to the training location, or a visit to a customer location.
- Ask that participants describe some role-modeling behavior in the organization that focuses on specific actions related to the skill lesson.

Videos: Using Them to Their Best Advantage

Video can be a wonderful tool to use in teaching, but its value and effectiveness can be diminished by incorrect use.

- Instead of showing videos in their entirety, show clips. Pick a scene to model a behavior or its opposite. Ask people what they liked or how they might do things differently.
- Develop a case study, and use a clip to illustrate one aspect.
- Make videos available to people afterward in the resource library,

should they want to review the materials, show them to colleagues, or see the entire program.

- Determine the appropriate use for the video:
  - ✓ What am I trying to achieve through showing this video? What are the desired learning outcomes?
  - ✓ Where might this video best be placed?
    - To initiate discussion?
    - To summarize learning?
    - As part of a case study?
  - ✓ Integrate the video into the training design.
  - ✓ Where appropriate, set out the desired learning outcomes in advance of viewing the video.
  - ✓ Design questions related to the video, for response by individuals or teams.
- Always remember to:
  - ✓ View the video in advance of the program to ensure your own thorough knowledge of its key points.
  - ✓ Check video clarity, color, and sound just before the workshop.
  - ✓ Beware of videos where fashions or verbal expressions are considerably out of date; trainees will be easily distracted by these discrepancies.
- When considering renting or purchasing a video, keep in mind:
  - ✓ There are excellent previewing services available. Use them rather than relying on catalog summaries.
  - ✓ Look in your local library for low-cost alternatives for borrowing.
  - ✓ Send out an SOS to your organization asking whether there are any good videos available on a specific topic. Many managers have a wide selection of videos sitting unused in cabinets.
  - ✓ Other organizations you deal with may have good videos that you can borrow in exchange for some other service.
  - ✓ Do your math when deciding to rent or buy. If you intend to use the video for several sessions, it is usually more cost-effective to buy it outright.

Producing a Video In-House

- You may have the facilities to produce a video in-house, even with a limited budget. In-house video production for training works best for:

- ✓ Executive messages (including an endorsement of a training program)
- ✓ A question-and-answer session that discusses some teaching points in the course
- ✓ Demonstration of equipment-repair techniques
- ✓ A visual tour of a plant or production facility
- Making an in-house video without the benefit of a professional scriptwriter can be accomplished by using one of these alternatives:
  - ✓ Write the initial drafts yourself, and have a professional edit your text.
  - ✓ Send someone from your organization for training to learn the basics.
- Getting time from a senior person to endorse your program can be difficult. You will make your task easier if you:
  - ✓ Choose to work with people who are committed to the message, even though they may not be at the highest level.
  - ✓ Prepare them in advance for the time requirement, with the understanding that seldom is the first take satisfactory.
  - ✓ Get their input into the content, so that they appear genuinely happy to make whatever pitch it is.
  - ✓ Prepare the set beforehand to make sure that little time is wasted when they arrive.
- A lengthy speech filmed with one camera can be improved by:
  - ✓ Suggesting to the executive that it be edited to include highlights
  - ✓ Interspersing the view of the executive with clips of people and places that might illustrate his or her points visually
- Make use of professional actors if:
  - ✓ You need to save time.
  - ✓ You have the budget.
  - ✓ Your organization is fairly large and the person you are portraying is not well known.
  - ✓ The job you are showing is done by several people.
  - ✓ The topic is generic and applies throughout the organization (for example, health and safety).
- *Caution:* Mixing professional actors with staff is rarely a good idea because the presence of the professionals will intimidate your employees. You can use in-house people and have a professional narrator do commentaries and background voices.
- The choice of where to shoot will be influenced by:
  - ✓ The budget

✓ The ability to build or create authentic scenes away from work
✓ The convenience of having all the equipment in one place and not having to travel from place to place
✓ The possibility of interference of people and noises on-site

---

Dealing with Difficult Behavior

> *"Everyone is entitled to be stupid, but some abuse the privilege."*
>
> —UNKNOWN

I t is said that trainers have to deal with three types of people:

1. *Learners*, who want to be there and get as much as they can from the session
2. *Vacationers*, who want to have as much fun and free time as possible
3. *Prisoners*, who resent being there

A training session can be thrown off course by a variety of uncooperative behaviors. Here are the most frequent types and ideas for dealing with each.

The Negative Person

- Most often the frustration is legitimate. Your goal is to help the participant to find a good reason for being at the training session.
- Allow the person to vent and get any frustrations off his or her chest. Then you can decide whether to:
  ✓ Empathize and ask if you can move on
  ✓ Empathize and determine if the issue needs to be dealt with right away

✓ Empathize and offer to deal with the issue later or at the end of
    the meeting
- Control your response. You have many options including:
    ✓ Not taking the issue personally.
    ✓ Not getting drawn into an argument.
    ✓ Not showing anger. Keep calm (outwardly), and keep a straight
        face. If you show that the negative person is getting to you, you
        will be demonstrating publicly a lack of ability to deal with the
        situation.
    ✓ Canvassing the opinions of others in the workshop, especially if
        the person is making wild, exaggerated statements. This way the
        person will be made to understand that his or her opinions do
        not represent those held by others in the workshop.
    ✓ Asking the frustrated learner to give you ideas as to how to deal
        with the difficulties.
    ✓ Calling a time-out and regroup. Collect your thoughts and com-
        posure. Take the time to revise your strategy to deal with the
        problem.
    ✓ Letting peer pressure deal with the culprit.
    ✓ Addressing antagonistic questions as serious and legitimate.
        Simply answer them and move on.

The Overly Talkative Participant

- This individual is well intentioned but insensitive to the needs of
    others' expectations of equal airtime. So alleviate the situation by:
    ✓ Establishing a learning contract at the beginning of the session
        that includes ensuring that everyone has equal opportunity to
        participate.
    ✓ Reminding the person diplomatically of the contract and the im-
        portance of getting other perspectives.
    ✓ Jumping in when the person stops to catch his or her breath, and
        echo the person's comments. For example, say, "So what I'm
        hearing is that (. . .) Thank you. Now who else has something to
        add that has not already been covered?"
    ✓ Doing a round robin to ensure equal opportunity to use the
        available time. Say, "Let's go around the table and get one idea
        from each person. If you don't have an idea, just say *pass.*"

✓ Avoiding frequent eye contact with the person. This only serves to invite additional comment.

✓ Directing questions to people other than the talkative person.

✓ Discussing the issue with the person privately at a break, and stressing the importance of letting everyone have a chance to respond.

The Rambler

• This person engages in conversations that hop from topic to topic without a specific focus or point. So help the discussion get back on track quickly by:

✓ Summarizing the person's ideas in order to bring clarity. Then, after getting an agreement that you have understood them, move on.

✓ Emphasizing the importance of staying on schedule.

✓ Recording the ideas offered on a flip chart. This will reduce repetition and force the person to organize his or her thoughts.

Preparation Strategies

• Your best strategy for anticipated difficulties during training is getting good information beforehand about the group and its dynamics:

✓ Review the evaluations from other groups to whom you've given the course. Pay particular attention to which topics generated the least interest or most confusion, and analyze why.

✓ Talk with the manager or managers of the participants. Find out as much as you can about learning styles, communication styles, and general enthusiasm about the training.

✓ Get a sense about other organization issues that may be playing on the trainees' minds—for example, downsizing, new performance measures, or upcoming management changes.

✓ Develop a demographic profile of the group to see whether there is some natural tension among participants already (for example, managers attending along with their direct reports).

✓ Conduct an informal telephone survey with some participants to understand their expectations and previous positive and negative training experiences.

✓ Talk to someone who has trained the group before. What are this person's observations?

Resistance to Training

B efore you can teach people anything, you may have to overcome their resistance; otherwise, you will feel as if you are pushing a rope. Here are the main sources of resistance and some useful strategies to counter them.

Source 1: Group Resistance. Cooperating with the trainer might be viewed as being a traitor if the objectives of the training appear contrary to the interests of the group. A teamwork program, for example, might be seen as a productivity enhancement program that would cause layoffs. In the event that participants are ganging up against you, you should:

✓ Not avoid the issue but rather tackle it head-on.
✓ Deal with it whenever you feel no meeting of the minds.
✓ Not single anyone out.
✓ Point out your observations and feelings, and ask for confirmation that there is a problem.
✓ Show your interest by listening and not being defensive.
✓ Engage the group in finding ways to deal with the problem.
✓ Separate issues that can be dealt with inside the workshop from those that can only be fixed outside (if at all).
✓ Deal with matters that can be fixed and over which people in the workshop have control. Also, ask people to take responsibility for the other issues outside the session at a later time.

Source 2: Resistance to Change. People who have been working in certain ways for years may find it difficult to accept radically different approaches. Try the following strategies:

✓ Encourage people to make smaller changes.
✓ Have them practice new skills without any chance of losing face or being ridiculed.
✓ Find the cause of the resistance and encourage discussion of it.
✓ Demonstrate the new behavior or skill yourself, and get feedback about positive impacts.
✓ Canvas the opinions of those who are in favor of the change.
✓ Provide rewards for changed behavior, no matter how slight.
✓ Empathize with people's unwillingness to try to change.

Source 3: Fear of Appearing Foolish. Doing something wrong in front of others might cause embarrassment. A person might refuse to experiment rather than seem incompetent. Some strategies to adopt include the following:

✓ Develop an understanding up-front about people's needing to take risks.
✓ Do not allow ridicule.
✓ Laugh at your own mistakes if they occur.
✓ Keep the session light with lots of humor to create a relaxed, more permissive environment.

Source 4: Unclear Goals and Objectives. Often people are sent to a workshop with inaccurate or no information about the course objectives. They may become openly hostile if they find themselves hostage to something they have limited use for, or they may become withdrawn and uncooperative, taxing the patience of all those in the room.

✓ Don't confront them in the class. You do not need a standoff that will produce a win-lose or lose-lose outcome. Speak to them at the first break. Empathize with their frustration, and ask them for help with a solution.
✓ Offer to help with their issues by adding *their* learning needs to the agenda or giving them an opportunity to share their experiences and knowledge with others.
✓ Offer to help later if their needs cannot be met during the session.
✓ Renegotiate the learning objectives, and do your best to modify the program if you feel that your objectives and those of most of

the trainees are not in accord. If this is difficult, at least give people a chance to vent, and listen with empathy.

✓ If the program is mandatory, consider shortening it in return for participants' cooperation.

Keeping Trainees Focused

> *"Learning is not attained by chance, it must be sought for with ardor and attended to with diligence."*
>
> —ABIGAIL ADAMS
> Wife of U.S. President John Adams

Whether a course is held as a public forum or at an employee's worksite, all facilitators acknowledge that keeping trainees inside the training room is a chronic challenge. Today's technology—cellular phones, pagers, wireless pda's—exacerbates the challenge by increasing the likelihood of distractions.

- There are three reasons that trainees excuse themselves from training:

    1. Business emergencies (clients, bosses, or colleagues contact them)
    2. Personal emergencies (family illness, midday appointments)
    3. Boredom (trainees may plead business or personal emergencies)

Here are some techniques for minimizing trainee exodus and time lost to catch-up training:

Prior to the Workshop

- Speak to participants before the class—particularly if it is being conducted on-site—to discuss the importance of staying in the class throughout the course. Stress the following items:

- ✓ The problem of gaps in their learning if they leave
- ✓ The possibility of letting their teammates down in group activities
- ✓ The creation of a precedent for others who might feel tempted to leave at will
- ✓ The importance of demonstrating commitment to the program
- ✓ How people might question their organization skills and ability to delegate
- Speak to the participants' managers. Seek their support to:
  - ✓ Arrange cover for the trainee
  - ✓ Not bother the trainee about minor issues
  - ✓ Stress the importance of the program to the trainee

At the Workshop

- *Always* start the course on time. This is a clear message that tardiness after breaks and lunch will not be rewarded by late starts.
- Start by discussing a code of conduct for interruptions. Involve trainees in identifying what are legitimate excuses.
- Recruit a senior manager to kick off the course to emphasize the importance of professional behavior.
- Secure group consensus about the use of cellular phones and wireless technology.
- Agree on break times, and stick to those times as diligently as possible.
- Set up a message board outside the classroom.
- Set rules for participants' reentry into the classroom.
- Make yourself available at lunch breaks for catch-up exercises for those who had to leave briefly.
- Limit the likelihood of trainees' choosing to leave the classroom by:
  - ✓ Designating learning buddies who are accountable for catch-up information if their buddies must come and go.
  - ✓ Monitoring group energy and interest; take five-minute time-outs if interest is waning.
  - ✓ Setting an incentive for no interruptions (for example, finishing a half hour earlier than scheduled).
  - ✓ Changing the composition of breakout teams regularly during the day. New teammates can be energizing.

✓ Ensuring that there is frequent group participation; one-way discussions can be boring.

✓ Using videos (one for each half-day session) to generate renewed interest and discussion.

✓ Inviting executives to drop in during the day, and letting trainees know they're coming. Most trainees like their supervisors to see them actively involved in learning.

✓ Sticking to the agenda to reinforce a sense of professionalism in the classroom.

✓ Changing the venue for breakout exercises. A change of scene can counter boredom. Creative alternatives include being out of doors, in the hotel restaurant, or the organization stockroom.

✓ Closing the session with a special guest or corporate executives.

✓ Suggesting that trainees ask for the group's permission to leave the room for things other than restroom breaks. (This may not work in all cases; some people might find this approach childish.)

• Trainees are more inclined to be timely when they feel that they are learning. A trainer can show his or her interest in the amount of learning taking place. The following suggestion can help a trainer do this:

✓ Put a piggy bank in front of each person or one at each table.

✓ Give each person twenty pennies.

✓ Ask people to put a penny in the piggy bank each time they learn something new or interesting.

• Giving people the assurance that their needs will be met is an added inducement to stay. You can do this by:

✓ Leaving a blank page on the wall, called *Parking Lot*, in which issues unrelated to your topic are listed for discussion at a specified time.

✓ Giving each person sticky notes to write questions on. These can be put on a flip-chart page, prominently displayed.

Flip Chart Do's and Don'ts

F lip charts are still every trainer's best friend. They provide the lowest-cost tool with the highest impact (and no downtime!). Flip charts are readily available wherever you go, portable, and easy to use.

- The following tips will help a trainer to make the best use of a flip chart:
    - ✓ Write in bold, capital letters.
    - ✓ Use dark colors for words—black or dark blue is best—and alternate the colors for each point when doing a long list.
    - ✓ Number each point for easy reference.
    - ✓ Use colors for highlighting, underlining, and bullets.
    - ✓ Emphasize headings by writing them larger, using a different color, or underlining.
    - ✓ Keep one idea per page.
    - ✓ Post key ideas on the walls for easy reference.
    - ✓ Precut masking tape, and stick the pieces on the legs of the flip chart stand. Use them to post pages on the walls. Put the tape on the side of the pages, not the top, so all you have to do is tear and post.
    - ✓ Use diagrams and flowcharts to increase understanding.
    - ✓ Add pictures where possible. Remember that a picture is worth a thousand words!
    - ✓ Add reminders of the points you want to make by writing them in pencil on the appropriate flip-chart page. You will be able to see the information, but your audience won't. They will be astonished at your familiarity with so many facts and figures.
    - ✓ Attach a label to key pages if you want to refer back to an idea without thumbing through all the pages. You can (1) put a masking tape tab with details written on it or (2) color-code certain topics so that related subjects have a single color.
    - ✓ If you're going to draw a model or diagram, predraw it in light pencil (so only you can see it).
    - ✓ Always print clearly.
- Here are some don'ts:

✓ Don't block the flip chart when you are writing on it. Stand to the side.

✓ Don't talk at the flip chart as you are writing on it.

✓ Avoid using markers made from strong chemicals. The writing may bleed through the flip-chart paper.

✓ Beware of using red or green; 7 percent of the population is color-blind and have trouble distinguishing these colors.

Overhead Projector Do's and Don'ts

U sing the overhead projector correctly will add to the effectiveness of your presentation and message. Here are key ideas to help you.

- Check that the lightbulb is working. If your machine uses two lightbulbs in case one fails, check both.
- Learn how to use the overhead *before* your presentation. Different manufacturers have different switching systems.
- Focus the machine before you start to avoid the embarrassment of an indistinct picture. Make sure the picture is exactly on the screen.
- Clean the faceplate to remove dirt that will project on the screen.
- Number your transparencies, and have them laid out in front of you so you can see the next one before you get to it. This will help you to bridge the information from one transparency to the next, thereby knitting your presentation together.
- Use the "four-by-four" rule: Try not to exceed four lines per transparency and more than four words per line.
- Don't use your fingers to point to items on your transparency. Your hand might shake, making people aware of your nervousness. Use a stir stick or pencil (not a round one, which will roll).
- Show all the information first. Then refer to each item one by one.
- Don't block the audience's view of the visuals.
- Your overheads will be effective if you follow these guidelines:
  ✓ Use bold, capital letters.

✓ Avoid using red: this color is more difficult to read than any other color.
✓ Add or change color for headings and bullets.
✓ Emphasize headings by making them larger.
✓ Use only one idea or concept per transparency.
✓ Use diagrams and graphs to increase audience understanding.
✓ Add pictures to create an impression as well as increase understanding.
✓ Keep each transparency simple.

Activities and Exercises

"If a man insisted always on being serious, and never allowed himself a bit of fun and relaxation, he would go mad or become unstable without knowing it."

—HERODOTUS
Greek Historian and Author of
The Histories

Games are used often in training sessions to demonstrate specific teaching principles through highly participative and nonthreatening exercises. Games work best when they use techniques and tools that are not related to the participants' working environment.

• There are many games available in packaged formats and in specialized training guides.
• In selecting or designing games, ensure that any game is consistent with adult learning principles. The games must be interesting, challenging, and not embarrassing for the participants. The game should continue for as long as it takes to ensure that participants have learned from it.
• Games should encourage healthy and humorous competition, which should acknowledge winners but never denigrate losers.

- Target games to the maturity and comfort level of the participants (not everyone likes to be blindfolded).
- Games should be directly related to a specific teaching principle in the lesson plan rather than to generic principles or observations.
- Ensure that the game is reasonably novel for the participants. For example, many people have already been through simulated survival exercises.
- The intended outcomes or conclusions should not be predictable or obvious from the outset (for example, that ten hands work faster than two hands).
- If the group is being divided into teams, make sure that the teams are small enough so all members can participate.
- Instructions should be clearly stated or written. Constant requests for clarification detract from the energy of the learning opportunities.
- The learning observations should refer to the process as well as the outcome.
- Allow ample time for debriefing the learning outcomes.
- Ensure that the time allotted for the game is adequate; otherwise, clock watching will compromise the learning.

Here are some suggestions for games that relate to typical course objectives.

Teamwork Practices

- Use puzzles or crosswords that are missing some important pieces or clues. This game encourages listening and questioning skills at the same time as it demonstrates the importance of collaboration.
- Charge each group with the task of designing the "perfect" restaurant menu (or holiday resort). During the debriefing, have groups discuss how they arrived at consensus and handled differences.

Time-Management Techniques

- As a variation on standard "in-basket" exercises, design a list of activities that describe preparations for a vacation or spring housecleaning, and ask participants to prioritize the list.

- Hand out copies of the daily newspaper, and give each participant ten minutes to prepare a one-page summary of the news. The participants who prepared the most concise yet comprehensive summaries then describe their methods.

Customer Service

- Have participants lunch at a local fast-food restaurant. Have each person report back on the most and least appealing features of the service they received. Compare and discuss preferences and differences.
- Have three or four participants draw up a list of features for their perfect car. Divide the class into sales teams who interview each "buyer." Compare how long it takes each team to develop buyer profiles.

Brainstorming and Creativity Exercises

- Give each team some modeling clay. Ask them to design a sculpture that represents a particular theme, such as freedom or love.
- Cut out pictures of products from a magazine. Ask each team to design an advertising slogan for each product.

Computer-Projected Presentations

"Any sufficiently advanced technology is indistinguishable from magic."

—ARTHUR C. CLARKE
Science Fiction Writer and Author

Projecting images from your laptop has quickly become the preferred method of trainers when sharing information. As training becomes more high tech, there is a danger of overdazzling an audience instead of connecting with them. The following tips can enhance your message by using computer projection equipment:

- Prepare your slides with similar principles that you used with your overhead projector. Remember: Your slides are meant to complement your voice and animation, not replace it. Therefore:
  - ✓ For the most part, keep your slides consistent—changing them each time to different animations will detract from the message and have people focusing on the technology instead. Most software programs have the ability to add many sounds, but few have any relevance to the message. Cars screeching, guns blazing, and bells ringing may be appropriate perhaps once a day, and then only for very special reasons.
  - ✓ Ensure that your pictures complement the message. Avoid using common stick people. Instead, look to the Internet for new clips that enhance the message.
  - ✓ Maintain the 5 & 5 rule—no more than five sentences (short) and five words per line. Less is better.
- Get yourself a remote control so that you can walk around the room without needing to stand at the computer and press keys for the next slide.
- Design slides to be pleasant to see and easy to read. Use dark writing on a white background or light (white or yellow) writing on a dark background—both work well. With beautiful colors and scenic backgrounds, make a choice that complements your message.
- Ensure that your slides are compatible with your workbook. If the sequence is different, the participants will be confused.
- Make sure that your LCD projector is powerful enough to project a clear picture, particularly in a light room.
- Test the equipment early. Some venues have only first-generation LCDs, which may be incompatible with your latest software. A smart technician may be able to help you by doing the following:
  - ✓ Reducing your resolution (resulting in a fuzzy picture)
  - ✓ Using a copy of your presentation in their computer
  - ✓ Toggling the Fn (function) key with the F5 or F8 CRT/LCD key, depending on the computer you're using, which alternates projection from your computer screen only, to the projector only, to both.
- When you are not using the projector, turn it off by pressing the B (black) or W (white) key on your computer. This way people will be looking at you and not the screen.

- Never read your presentation off the screen. In fact, never read the lines on your slides! Your audience is literate and capable of doing so. Instead, before a new slide is shown, provide an introductory comment to it such as "Now I'm going to show you the four most important ideas . . ." Then, after the slide is projected, and people have had a chance to read the ideas, ask questions that will challenge them to understand the ideas. You could, for example, ask "Which do you think is the best idea?" or "Which tip would work best for you?"
- Use the feature that displays one line at time sparingly. Use it only for key slides where each line is important and you want to discuss the lines one at a time. Doing this too often allows you too much control and leaves the audience with a sense of powerlessness.
- Where possible, use your computer to project video. The impact is greater because of the large screen.

Presentation Skills

"The only thing you can do better than anyone else is to be yourself."

—KATHY CONWAY
Author of *The Trainer's Tool Kit*

Connecting with people in a meaningful way is particularly important for trainers. Presenting to groups scares the living daylights out of most people. Needless to say, this is not a skill that is developed overnight, or at a one-day workshop. It is a craft that one improves gradually over time by constantly working on it. Your primary task in presenting information is to improve understanding, transfer information, and encourage retention by making the process interesting, challenging, and fun. The following tips can help you to do just that:

- Relax, and welcome people into the meeting room. Show your confidence and approachability with a firm handshake and a smile.

- Welcome the trainees officially when they are seated. Let them know what to expect. Remind them of your agenda, the expected outcome, the amount of time you intend to take, and any break times. Tell them you will pass out copies of the presentation *after* you have made it. Also, let them know where the rest rooms and fire exits are.
- Start off with as much impact as possible. Present a challenge or recall a story that will move your audience.
- Ask rhetorical questions from time to time. Challenge your audience. Conduct periodic polls by asking a question that needs a show of hands for an answer.
- When you conduct a question-and-answer session, focus on those people who have demonstrated from the start of the session that they are likely to be constructive and positive.
- Keep the presentation to the point. Don't cover material that the audience already knows. Focus on new information.
- Do not read word-for-word from your notes, slides, or overheads. The audience can do that too. Give people a chance to read each visual; then paraphrase the content, stressing key points.
- Provide a bridging comment between each overhead or slide to knit your presentation together.
- Keep eye contact with your audience.
- Scan the audience, looking at each person for three to five seconds if your audience is small.
- Don't read off the screen or turn your back on the audience.
- Maintain attention by:
  - ✓ Changing the pace of presentation from time to time
  - ✓ Doing something different at least every seven minutes (for example, ask questions, poll the audience, complete questionnaires, do group work)
  - ✓ Modulating your voice, speaking loudly and then softly, quickly and then deliberately
  - ✓ Animating your facial expressions and gestures
  - ✓ Gesturing appropriately
- Move around the room, getting closer to your audience when they ask questions. Staying behind a podium will build a wall between you and your audience.
- Grab the audience's attention when you feel it is waning. Consider doing the following:

✓ Challenge your audience by starting off with one of the five Ws and an H.
  - Who would like . . . ?
  - What would be the one . . . ?
  - When was the last time you . . . ?
  - Where is the best place you . . . ?
  - Why is it that . . . ?
  - How can you . . . ?
✓ Quote a shocking statistic, or take a controversial stance.
- Use humor. But do so only if you are good at telling jokes and only if the story is relevant to the subject. A failed joke will just increase tension and your embarrassment. The best humor is a story that is self-deprecating. This type of story will not only amuse your audience but develop a link with them, since you are signaling to them that you are "normal." Never tell a joke that could offend.
- Use gestures to increase your effectiveness.
  ✓ Open your arms to the audience, when appropriate, as if to embrace them.
  ✓ Keep your arms at your sides when you are not using them.
  ✓ Keep arm gestures between your waist and shoulder.
  ✓ Avoid quick and jerky gestures, which give the impression of nervousness.
  ✓ Vary your gestures to suit your message. A continuous single gesture will be distracting.
  ✓ Don't overuse gestures, or they will lose their impact.
- Use as much of the space in front of your audience as possible. Avoid standing behind a lectern. Involve your audience. For instance, take a poll, ask for opinions, or find out if anyone can relate to the example you have described. This interaction will show you are interested in and care about the opinions of your audience members.
- Improve retention and interest:
  ✓ Share anecdotes that illustrate key points. People will visualize the story and remember it.
  ✓ Use analogies—for example, "Working without goals is like traveling without a map."
  ✓ Use metaphors. Saying, "That salesperson is like a fox" is more effective than saying, "He is clever."
  ✓ Use props to add impact. Hold up articles, books, or magazines when you quote from recognized experts.

- Use your voice to add impact.
  - ✓ Change your voice modulation. Speak quickly or slowly, loudly or softly, for brief periods.
  - ✓ Generally speak a little louder than you do normally.
  - ✓ Pause before or after a key thought.
  - ✓ If you are not sure what to say, pause briefly to collect your thoughts, but *without saying "um" or "ah."*
- Project positive body language, which will convey your confidence to the audience.
  - ✓ Stand erect and tall, and push your chest out.
  - ✓ Avoid putting your hands on one or both hips, a stance that projects arrogance.
  - ✓ A protrusion of one hip signals that you don't want to be there. So does a prolonged eye blink.
  - ✓ Maintain steady eye contact with your audience. Fast-shifting eyes indicate a lack of certainty.
- End with a challenge that leaves the audience with something to think about.

Facilitator Do's and Don'ts

> *"Make sure you have finished speaking before your audience has finished listening."*
>
> —DOROTHY SAMOFF
> Actor

Most trainees help the facilitator to succeed. The following advice from the pros can help any facilitator to get the group on his or her side.

DO'S

- Shake hands with participants as they enter the room to establish a one-on-one relationship.

- Substitute the word *and* for the word *but* whenever possible. For example: "You've made an interesting point, and your colleagues disagree with you." You've lost nothing in your message, yet have reduced the risk of alienating the trainee.
- Lean into the group when the discussion gets heated. It's a sign of respect, if not necessarily agreement.
- Ask for suggestions from the group in answering difficult questions.
- Nod your head as you listen to suggestions, to emphasize acute listening and interest.
- Walk around the room as much as possible, so that you are close to people when engaging them in discussion.
- Monitor the group carefully to gauge energy levels. Call for breaks when you sense lagging attention.
- Use participants' names as often as possible.
- Make it clear through examples and language that you respect the intelligence of the group members.
- Establish at the start what kinds of discussions and issues are unrelated and inappropriate for this session. Examples would be salaries and benefits or personality issues.

It is easy for facilitators to dig themselves into a hole and then find it difficult to extricate themselves. The following don'ts are from real pros about facilitator behavior, i.e. trainees themselves:

Don'ts

- Exaggerated or insincere enthusiasm about delivering the training
- Numerous personal anecdotes, especially when they are unrelated to the topic
- Inadequate preparation
- Delaying the start of training to accommodate latecomers
- Staying rooted to one spot
- Not managing participants who monopolize conversation
- Talking down to the group
- Conducting childish games
- Reading verbatim from overheads rather than expanding on key points
- Not finishing the training on time

Top 10 Tips for Trainers

Trainers should never take their ability to wing it as a guarantee of success. Every session is a new challenge. Focusing on key tasks will ensure success in the classroom.

1. Stick to an agenda.
   ✓ Everyone needs a plan. The agenda is the road map that will lead to the achievement of the learning objectives.
   ✓ Discuss and display the agenda and outline times for each section.
   ✓ Point out where you are from time to time.
2. Focus on the learning objectives. Keep your eye on the ball. If you allow the workshop to stray too far and for too long, you will disappoint participants. Not using the tools on the job will produce no measurable performance improvement—the most important indicator of success.
3. Train adults as adults. The days of show-and-tell, with the presumption that the audience is ignorant, are long gone. A good facilitator will:
   ✓ Challenge participants
   ✓ Respect them
   ✓ Listen to them, knowing that they have much to contribute
   ✓ Allow them to influence the process and content of the session
   ✓ Give them the opportunity to learn through self-discovery
   ✓ Provide a safe learning environment
   ✓ Give feedback professionally
4. Ensure equal participation. It is easy to allow the few confident extroverts to dominate discussions. You can ensure that the time is shared equally by:
   ✓ Using a round robin, giving everyone the opportunity to comment, one at a time.
   ✓ Avoiding eye contact with those who want to continue to dominate the discussion.
   ✓ Asking the quieter people questions directly.
   ✓ Privately making people aware of their tendency to dominate. Ask for their help in drawing others out.

✓ Thanking people for their willingness to contribute, then saying, "Let's get some other opinions."

5. Deal with dysfunctional behavior. There is seldom a workshop in which at least one person does not seem disinterested, hostile, or withdrawn. These behaviors can be ignored only at your peril. In all cases, intervene whenever the behavior is affecting others in the workshop:

   ✓ Approach the person.
   - Make the person aware of your concern.
   - Focus on the problem. Do not make a personal attack.
   - Listen to any complaints the person may have.
   - Offer help, insofar as you may have control over the problem.
   - Ask for the person's cooperation by appealing to his or her maturity.

6. Give your best. People have high expectations for training delivery. You need to give 100 percent of your enthusiasm and knowledge to be appreciated. If things aren't going as planned, though, and you've tried to rectify the situation:

   ✓ Don't apologize for any shortfalls. Your participants may not even be aware that there is a problem.
   ✓ Be assertive in dealing with the problem. Weakness and a lack of decisiveness on your part will erode trainees' confidence in the program.

7. Review the agenda. At the end of each day or the beginning of the next day, review what you have covered. This can be done by having a:

   ✓ Brief summary
   ✓ Round robin, asking people to call out the most useful thing that they have learned that day

8. Listen to the trainees:

   ✓ Never work in a vacuum. You ignore participants at your peril.
   ✓ Listen to what they say and how they say it.
   ✓ Observe body language. Negative signs may include:
   - Rolling eyes
   - Avoiding eye contact
   - Crossed arms and legs
   - Folding arms behind the head and leaning back
   - Leaving the room frequently
   ✓ When you notice a problem, listen closely to questions so that you can fully answer them. You can do this best by:

- Rephrasing their questions, to confirm your understanding
- Not filling your mind with a rebuttal or an alternative idea as someone is speaking.

9. Provide a safe environment. People need to practice skills before they can be expected to use them in their work environment. You can create a sense of security by:
   ✓ Using humor and self-deprecation
   ✓ Stressing the importance of learning from feedback
   ✓ Being a role model, then inviting feedback on how you are doing
   ✓ Establishing a learning contract that stresses the importance of helping one another through feedback

10. Have fun. People learn best when the environment is relaxed and they are enjoying themselves. This will not detract from the importance of the task at hand. You can help to keep a smile on participants' faces by:
    ✓ Telling appropriate jokes
    ✓ Laughing at yourself
    ✓ Illustrating theory with amusing anecdotes
    ✓ Using short activities that are fun
    ✓ Keeping an upbeat tempo
    ✓ Having fun yourself

Humor

"A sense of humor is part of the art of leadership, of getting along with people, of getting things done."

—DWIGHT D. EISENHOWER
Former U.S. President

The appropriate use of humor in training will get people relaxed and add to their enjoyment of the process. Use the following guidelines for incorporating humor:

- Use stories that are funny and that illustrate a teaching point you are covering.
- Use self-deprecating humor.
- Avoid using humor at anyone's expense or that may embarrass the organization.
- Never use humor that can be construed as racist or sexist in any way. Even in an all-male group, referring to women in a sexist manner will demonstrate a lack of professionalism and undermine your credibility.
- Avoid telling jokes if you are not good at it. It will cause you embarrassment and increase tension.
- Don't rely solely on your own repertoire of jokes to establish a sense of ease. Here are some ways to introduce some fun without performing:
  - ✓ Invite participants to start the session or a new module with their own best joke, and award a prize based on a group rating.
  - ✓ Establish an inventory of comic strips on overheads that can gently poke fun at certain common or organization occurrences.
  - ✓ Have participants talk about their worst customer service experience or "bad boss" stories if they relate to the lesson (rule out any experiences that refer to the current organization).
  - ✓ Have participants volunteer to describe their worst gaffe in trying to use a specific skill being taught. Give out a prize for the "best" gaffe.
  - ✓ Be on the lookout for quotes that point out certain absurdities about workplace behavior. Start a session or a module with an overhead with the appropriate quote, or include it in the training materials.
  - ✓ Use videos that have some sophisticated humor built into the teaching principles.
  - ✓ Hand out articles that have some humorous observations about certain workplace practices (for example, "What I Shouldn't Have Learned at My Corporate Retreat").
  - ✓ Consider case studies or role plays that include certain behaviors that participants can laugh at and identify with.
  - ✓ Use games that are sufficiently complex or intriguing to encourage participants to experiment with several different solutions. This typically causes people to laugh at some of their misguided attempts.

Diversity in the Classroom

W orkplace demographics can create challenges for trainers, especially those who believe that trainees share their perspectives, values, and backgrounds. Insensitivity will compromise trainers' professionalism and learning outcomes, too.

- Diversity encompasses the following areas:
  - ✓ Ethnic diversity
  - ✓ Cultural diversity
  - ✓ Gender ratios
  - ✓ Age distribution
  - ✓ Physical capabilities
  - ✓ Experience in the workplace
- Diversity in the classroom reflects the diversity in the customer base. Learning to understand and appreciate different perceptions about service and value has become a hallmark of successful companies.

The following guidelines can help ensure that your demeanor, lessons, and exercises communicate respect for all participants.

- Start sessions by encouraging everyone to participate in a brief introduction. This will give you a good sense of the communication styles, language fluency, and ease of the participants.
- During your introduction, ask participants to speak about their overall work experience. This is not only informative but also shows respect for all prior work experience.
- At the beginning of the session, offer to spend break time helping anyone who has difficulty with the lessons. This avoids embarrassing trainees who might feel belittled in dealing at greater length with an issue that they feel is easy or trivial for others yet difficult or important to them.
- Check beforehand whether there are special equipment or access requirements for some trainees.
- Avoid using examples or anecdotes that may not be meaningful to everyone, such as old TV programs or local history events.

- Don't use sexist language, such as referring to managers as "he" and assistants as "she."
- Change the composition of breakout teams regularly throughout the day to help participants hear many different points of view.
- If a trainee is lip-reading, always face him or her and speak clearly and slowly.
- Don't automatically speak louder or more slowly to someone with an accent. The person's hearing and comprehension may be just fine, and you run the risk of appearing condescending.
- Watch out for unwitting references to your own culture (for example, "going to church," "the Protestant work ethic," or "we all grew up knowing that").
- *Never* make a sexist or racist remark or joke, even if the group appears homogeneous. You can never be sure of individual backgrounds and sensitivities. More important, these comments are *always* inappropriate.
- Never acknowledge a racist or sexist remark from participants. Just ignore it. If someone persists, speak to the person privately at the first break.
- Monitor the group carefully to understand who is having difficulty understanding the lessons because of language barriers. Adjust your style accordingly.
- Be knowledgeable about religious holidays for all major groups, and avoid scheduling training on those days.
- Take religious dietary prohibitions and restrictions into account when arranging luncheon menus.
- Choose videos that reflect current workforce demographics.
- Respect participants' personal space. Not everyone is comfortable with a tap on the shoulder, an arm around the shoulder, or a group hug.
- Beware of physical exercises that may challenge or embarrass some participants.
- Be sensitive to the fact that there are hidden differences that people may not be willing to disclose (for example, sexual orientation, disabilities, or health conditions). Be sure the content and your comments respect these differences.

Post-Course Evaluation

"The greater danger for most of us lies not in setting our aim too high and falling, but in setting our aim too low and achieving our mark."

—MICHELANGELO BUONARROTI
Italian Sculptor, Painter, and Architect

As training budgets shrink and training needs escalate, most organizations are taking a longer-term view to measuring training results. Nevertheless, post-course evaluation forms remain an important resource in the overall evaluation process.

- The post-course evaluation is a customer satisfaction tool that should measure the following course elements:
  ✓ Meeting trainees' expectations
  ✓ Timeliness of the course
  ✓ Length of the course
  ✓ Organization and flow of lessons and materials
  ✓ Facilitation effectiveness
  ✓ Immediate learning outcomes
  ✓ Facility, location, and comfort of the room
  ✓ Quality of materials (for example, binders, handouts, or videos)
  ✓ Pacing
  ✓ Relevance of the lesson to the job
  ✓ Ability to use the skills on the job
  ✓ Relevance of the lesson to long-term professional development
  ✓ Suggestions about training material
  ✓ Suggestions about facilitator style
  ✓ Most relevant and least relevant lessons
  ✓ Food and accommodations
- The following suggestions can help you to develop a meaningful post-course evaluation form:
  ✓ Customize a standard form to take into account specific objectives and conditions for the training. The more relevant the form is, the more likely that it will be completed.
  ✓ Use a satisfaction scale of 1 to 6 instead of 1 to 5. This scale

provides more meaningful gradations and avoids the widespread tendency to assign a 3 rating (which tells you little).

✓ Use a mixture of open and closed questions—for example, "Would you recommend the course to others?"; "Why or why not?"; or "List three things you have learned."

✓ Ask for overall ratings for both the course and the facilitator.

✓ Ask for comments about the level of participation.

✓ Balance questions that have positive and negative biases (for example, "most relevant/least relevant").

✓ Include time for completing evaluations in the course schedule.

✓ Solicit suggestions about ideal resources and conditions for implementing key learning principles.

✓ Use time frames to help you assess the application of the learning principles ("I expect to use my new skills: (a) immediately, (b) in three months, (c) in six months").

✓ Commit to sending a summary of the evaluations to all participants. This will underscore the importance you place on their feedback.

✓ Names and other identifying information should be optional.

✓ Ask for suggestions about designing an even more useful evaluation form. Most people enjoy the opportunity to be creative and are pleased when their ideas are sought.

✓ Do a brief evaluation at the end of the first day to see if you are on track, especially if the course is several days in length.

✓ The post-course evaluation form should be easy to read, easy to answer, and provide information that prepares you for more in-depth and long-term course effectiveness indicators. A sample is provided in Exhibit 7.

Exhibit 7. Example of evaluation sheet.

You are my client and I value your feedback. Please rate the workshop on each criterion listed below:

Workshop Process	Exceeded Expectations	Met Expectations	Needs Improvement	Not Applicable
Workshop organization	θ	θ	θ	θ
Presentation level	θ	θ	θ	θ
Quality of written materials	θ	θ	θ	θ
Activities and involvement	θ	θ	θ	θ
Visual aids	θ	θ	θ	θ
Presentation				
Presentation style	θ	θ	θ	θ
Facilitator's knowledge of subject	θ	θ	θ	θ
Clarity of the message	θ	θ	θ	θ
Handling of questions	θ	θ	θ	θ
Application				
Application to my job	θ	θ	θ	θ
Practicality of tools/ideas	θ	θ	θ	θ

How soon do you think you'll be using these new skills?

_____

_____

Suggestions for improvement of the program:

_____

_____

Other thoughts:

_____

_____

Please check the rating that best reflects your overall satisfaction with this session on a scale of 1 to 6.

Excellent = 6   Poor = 1

VII
Specialized Training Courses

Part VII contains practical do's and don'ts for training that are designed to fill a specific need. These courses are often conducted on an as-needed basis.

Orientation

"Begin at the beginning . . . and go on till you come to the end: then stop."

—LEWIS CAROLL
Alice's Adventures in Wonderland

It's in everybody's interest to start employees off on the right foot. An effective orientation will help get them up to speed and contributing quickly. The following guidelines will show you how to do it successfully whether you are a trainer or manager.

- Having hired the right person, it is in everyone's interest to promote the new employee's successful induction into the organization.
- Your program design will be influenced by the following four factors:
  1. *Budget*—how much money you have allocated to orientation
  2. *Geography*—number of different geographic locations
  3. *Volume*—number of new employees anticipated annually
  4. *Feedback*—from employees who have attended previous orientation programs
- Design your orientation program with the following factors in mind:
  ✓ Set standards for managers in orienting staff.
  ✓ Make the program easy for all managers to deliver.
  ✓ Stress the customers' perspective.
  ✓ List and discuss your organization's main competitors.
  ✓ Allow ample opportunities for new employees to ask questions.
  ✓ Deliver at least some parts of the program on the first day a new employee joins the organization.
  ✓ Create information booklets or brochures with important information for reference during and after the session.
  ✓ Consider the economics and usefulness of a new-employee info line.
- Avoid common mistakes when designing your program:
  ✓ Don't set complicated follow-up schedules, as they are difficult to maintain.

- ✓ Don't create expensive corporate videos if organization information is subject to change.
- ✓ Don't expect new employees to retain detailed information without printed reference material.
- ✓ Don't set unrealistic expectations and roles for your senior management team to deliver parts of the program if their schedules are subject to change.
- ✓ Don't delay the orientation program too long while waiting for a sizable group.
- Plan to ensure a successful integration of the new person:
  - ✓ Set up the new employee's workstation in advance.
  - ✓ Have someone greet the new employee on his or her arrival.
  - ✓ Post a notice on the bulletin board welcoming the employee and inviting others to do the same.
- Spend some time getting to know new associates. Learn about their work backgrounds, previous jobs, and likes and dislikes.
- Give the new employees information about the organization:
  - ✓ Organization history
  - ✓ The marketplace for its products or services
  - ✓ Customer overview
  - ✓ Organization structure and key people
  - ✓ Organization successes and challenges
  - ✓ Employee population
  - ✓ Standards of behavior
  - ✓ Performance standards, including hours of work
  - ✓ Documentation and information on salary and benefits
- Give new employees a tour of the facilities. Show them the key facilities, including the parking lot, rest rooms, cafeteria, and emergency exits.
- Review the organization's mission, values, and philosophy if these are available and documented. Discuss how the employees can contribute to the successful achievement of corporate goals.
- Show the new employees each department and how it relates to yours. Also show the major products and services. This information will give them the big picture so they can see how they fit.
- Conduct the orientation yourself, but consider giving each new employee a partner from another work area. This has the following important benefits:
  - ✓ It suggests that departments work together.
  - ✓ It establishes contacts with people in other areas.

✓ It improves communications between work areas.
✓ It stresses teamwork.
✓ It demonstrates your esteem for people outside your work area.
- To facilitate new employees' integration into the social fabric of the organization, provide a buddy who can act as a mentor when you are not available.
- Do not prejudice new employees about other people or departments by running them down. Allow new employees to form their own opinions based on their experiences.
- Establish an open-door policy so that employees have easy access to you when needed.
- Follow up regularly to see how new employees are doing. Praise their accomplishments to increase their confidence and sense of satisfaction at having joined the organization.
- Treat new employees as a resource. They will have a fresh perspective on ways of working. Be receptive to their ideas by showing your interest and, where possible, acting on their suggestions.
- Schedule a meeting about six weeks after the orientation to find out:
  ✓ How they are doing.
  ✓ What more you can do to help.
  ✓ Ways of improving the orientation process.
  ✓ Consider inviting a person's family or significant other for an orientation. You will demonstrate your interest in the total person.

Product Training

P roduct training, a core ingredient of most corporate training agendas, may be directed to an organization's employees or its customers.

- The need to conduct product training is usually ongoing, because:
  ✓ New products are introduced frequently.

✓ Products are changed.
✓ Employees are hired or promoted to positions where they will be marketing or selling products they are unfamiliar with.
✓ Product pricing changes.
- Internal processes that have an impact on requisitioning and product delivery change significantly over time.
- The following guidelines are important for designing and delivering product training:

Content

- Always include lessons that identify a product's features (its characteristics) and its benefits (how it helps the customer).
- Include information about your organization's big picture in selling the product—for example, intended market penetration, sales volumes, revenues, and profits.
- Describe and discuss any competitors' products.
- Present and discuss customer research, including feedback from focus groups, test marketing, and customer satisfaction studies.
- Develop clear guidelines for all internal processes that have an impact on selling or marketing the product, such as requisitioning, approval processes, and delivery arrangements.

Materials

- Secure all materials in easy-to-use binders that allow participants to add updates about features and processes.
- Divide the binder into easy reference components: pricing, benefits, marketplace analysis, and so forth.
- Distribute customer brochures and any other information that has been circulated publicly about the product, including news releases.
- Prepare a one-page summary with names and contact details for managers or specialists who can provide further information or hotline assistance.
- Design a chart that demonstrates the process flow as the product moves from the design stage through to customer delivery.

- Use pictures and charts to support teaching principles and examples whenever practical.
- Prepare a question-and-answer sheet that anticipates customer concerns.

Delivery

- Whenever possible, have samples of the product or a computer simulation for hands-on practice or demonstration.
- Use a ratio of three-to-one for discussion and practice versus lecture.
- Include realistic role plays as part of the practice. Use information from experienced sales and marketing staff for the role plays.
- Use short quizzes to gauge the audience's understanding after each short subject.
- Include a video that demonstrates sales, marketing, or listening skills to relieve the emphasis on specific product information as this will make, what is often a dry topic, more interesting.
- Keep an ongoing record of unexpected questions and concerns. Commit to a quick response to them.
- Be realistic about the course length. Don't cram too much information into a day. On the other hand, short modules over a period of time might compromise the course's impact and momentum.
- Solicit realistic input from participants about potential barriers to selling or marketing the product. Remember that equipping people to sell will not guarantee success.

Outdoor Training

More and more consultants in North America provide outdoor training experiences to individuals and organizations, attesting to the popularity of this form of training. Working and playing together within a different environment can bring about the following changes:

- *Changed Relationships.* People seem more prepared to deal with issues that are otherwise too uncomfortable to address at work, such as differences in workplace values.
- *Changed Mind-Set.* People might be less reliant on old paradigms and be more willing to change their mind-set.
- *Changed Perspective.* Experiencing coworkers in a new setting can lead to opportunities to gain new insight into and appreciation for one another.

- There are two types of outdoor training:
  1. Wilderness activities
  2. Outdoor activities in an urban area
- Wilderness activities can include activities such as the following:
  ✓ Hiking
  ✓ Canoeing
  ✓ White-water rafting
  ✓ Rock climbing
- Outdoor activities include:
  ✓ Exercises above ground level, usually using ropes
  ✓ Those that take place at ground level
- These activities can focus on individual achievement or the interaction of people in a team.
- The objectives for outdoor training vary but typically focus on the following:
  ✓ Team building
  ✓ Leadership development
  ✓ Development of self-confidence
  ✓ Problem solving
  ✓ Decision making
  ✓ Strengthening loyalty

The Process

- Setting up an outdoor program requires you to identify an issue that cannot easily or effectively be solved by another type of intervention. An example might be poor interpersonal chemistry between two people, loss of enthusiasm, or concerns about the future of the organization. If this is the case, seek a consultant who:

✓ Has a good track record with similar organizations
✓ Will help to customize the program to suit your staff
✓ Can design the program around key objectives
✓ Will provide any necessary follow-up assistance

The Training

- An effective outdoor program usually follows these steps:
    ✓ Begin with an icebreaker to get people as comfortable with each other as possible.
    ✓ Establish a learning contract, and set any guidelines to ensure health and safety.
    ✓ Take participants on a tour of the site to clear up any misconceptions they may have and increase everyone's comfort level.
    ✓ Conduct warm-up exercises, such as stretching, which will help to prevent injury.
    ✓ Conduct the designed exercises.
    ✓ Debrief, to enable the participants to share their thoughts and receive feedback.
    ✓ Connect the experiences to on-the-job realities.
- To bring closure to a day of challenge and physical exercise, the facilitator should debrief at the conclusion of each day. This review will be more successful if the facilitator-trainer follows these guidelines:
    ✓ Ask the participants if they would welcome feedback.
    ✓ Share all good and negative items, to ensure balance.
    ✓ Be as specific as possible, supporting the example with a video (if one is available).
    ✓ Provide every opportunity for the participants to identify their own problems and solutions.
    ✓ Stick to the facts without being judgmental and citing how you would have handled the situation.
- At the debriefing, a good facilitator will:
    ✓ Maintain some structure but loosen or tighten it as appropriate.
    ✓ Ensure that participants do not disclose inappropriate information (to the extent that that can be done).
    ✓ Respect confidentiality, as appropriate.

✓ Monitor that people do not get hurt if they naively disclose information that might otherwise come back to haunt them.

Conferences and Seminars

O rganizations deal daily with a wealth of literature that advertises professional development opportunities and requests from staff to attend.

- These venues include:
  - ✓ Industry events
  - ✓ Exhibitor events
  - ✓ Professional association conferences
  - ✓ Annual conventions
  - ✓ Special-interest networking forums
  - ✓ Executive development courses
  - ✓ External seminars for developing business skills
- Common issues for all organizations concerning these venues are:
  - ✓ Costs to attend
  - ✓ Selection of candidates
  - ✓ Benefits to the organization
- The following guidelines can be used to manage corporate funds and expectations for these forums:
  - ✓ Set annual budgets based on historical information and research about upcoming events.
  - ✓ Set corporate guidelines for attendance that emphasize business-based courses.
  - ✓ Identify courses that complement corporate succession planning processes, and prioritize candidates accordingly.
  - ✓ Request names of past participants from conference organizers, and do reference checking to help determine anticipated results from the session.
  - ✓ Take advantage of free presentations as often as is practical as sources of up-to-date information.

✓ Beware of events that are actually organized sales pitches (especially when there is a fee).

✓ Many conferences offer free tickets in exchange for services (for example, working the registration table or supplying a speaker from your company).

✓ Most conferences offer partial tickets for key events.

✓ Ensure that a list of participants and a summary of speakers' materials is included in the registration fee.

✓ Require your organization's attendee to prepare a synopsis of key information from the conference. Make course materials available for circulation and reference for other employees.

✓ Do follow-up networking with other participants to maximize your investment.

✓ Conduct ongoing research with other organizations to help set cost and attendance guidelines.

✓ Equip your organization's representatives with information kits about your products or services for networking.

Coach your organization's representatives about their role as ambassadors for your organization at these events.

VIII

Evaluating the Impact of Training on Performance Improvement

N o matter what the economic conditions, every dollar spent by organizations must be important in terms of producing a return on the investment. Training is one of the most difficult expenditures to measure and it is not surprising that it is usually the first cost to be cut when times are tough. Part VIII provides some answers to the vexing issue of justifying training expenditures.

Targeting the Right Results

"We know that half of the training investment pays off; trouble is that we don't know which half!"

—UNKNOWN

Training results are the positive changes in an employee's performance that occurred by acquiring new skills in a training program or by developing existing skills.

Training programs typically cover a variety of skills, which can make it difficult to identify one or two priority results. Results also depend on many factors, such as follow-up coaching, opportunities to apply skills, and training program design. Nevertheless, trainers and trainees will work together more effectively if they can relate course content to one or two specific performance results. The "right" results are the one or two changes in performance that are expected in return for the training investment, and link most closely to a needs analysis.

- Targeting the right results allows trainers, managers, and course designers to work toward common objectives by:
  - ✓ Identifying the right training audience
  - ✓ Aligning key learning objectives with results
  - ✓ Encouraging specific goals for post-course manager coaching
  - ✓ Establishing baselines for measuring training costs and benefits
- Targeted results, or performance improvements, are skills that are:
  - ✓ Specific to course content
  - ✓ Linked to realistic performance expectations
  - ✓ Within a trainee's scope of influence to apply and practice in his/her work environment
  - ✓ Can be improved with additional practice

Here are two steps to help you target expected results:

Step One: Performance Impact Stages

✓ Choose the statement that best describes the anticipated impact of skills training:

- Stage One—Employees will meet roles, goals, and standards for the current job.
- Stage Two—Employees will exceed roles, goals, and standards for the current job.
- Stage Three—Employees will prepare to meet roles, goals, and standards for advancement.

✓ After identifying the appropriate performance outcome, as indicated above, determine:
  - What specific changes in performance (R,G,S) are required or anticipated for the majority of trainees
  - Who will measure the change
  - What is a reasonable timeline for measuring change

Step Two: Identify the Impact

Use the results grid in Exhibit 8 to help your clients identify expected performance results. Some examples have been included in this illustration.

Levels of Evaluation

Training doesn't take place in a vacuum. It has a purpose to different stakeholders before, during, and after the session. Each stage and the benefits to each stakeholder should be measured, according to Donald Kirkpatrick, whose work on evaluating training has been adapted worldwide.[1]

- There are three reasons for evaluating a training program's effectiveness:
  1. To identify areas of improvement
  2. To determine whether a course should be continued or canceled
  3. To assess a program's role in an integrated training strategy

Exhibit 8. Results grid.

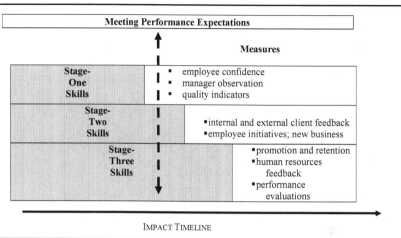

Notes:

1. The impact timeline indicates that impact increases depending on which stage the target audience is at, and that results may take longer to be felt in Stages 2 & 3.

2. The scope of people who have input for measuring performance increases as we move through the stages.

3. Skills will become more complex as you move through the stages.

Example: In the case of a customer service representative, the Results Grid can look like this:

- Kirkpatrick sets out four sequential levels in an evaluation process:
  - ✓ *Level One: Reaction.* Trainee's verbal and written feedback at the end of a course
  - ✓ *Level Two: Learning.* Trainee's understanding of the key learning principles
  - ✓ *Level Three: Behavior.* Observable application of the skill on the job
  - ✓ *Level Four: Results.* Quantifiable improvements in productivity that can be attributed to the training
- Here are some techniques for gathering useful information for all four levels of evaluation:

Level One: Reaction to the Training

- Design a user-friendly evaluation form that participants complete at the end of a training course. Leave room on it for comments and suggestions.
- Have participants rate and comment on the conditions of training, as well as the content (for example, facilities, length of course, course materials).
- Balance the questions between course content and course delivery (facilitation, materials, and so forth).
- Set aside time on the agenda for evaluations to ensure that all participants complete the form. It is extremely difficult to collect forms after the course.
- If the organization's culture values openness, encourage participants to put their name on the form.
- Change the order of questions on evaluation forms from course to course, and customize the content. Participants will consider their responses more carefully.
- Do some informal follow-up one to two weeks after the course. Ask participants if they have changed their mind about the evaluation they submitted.

Level Two: Learning/Understanding

- Determine whether the course was intended to change:
  - ✓ Attitudes

✓ Skills
✓ Knowledge
✓ A combination of these factors

- Use preseminar tests or quizzes to gauge the level of skills, knowledge, or attitudes before the training.
- Design a post-seminar test to determine new levels of skills, knowledge, or attitudes. Have participants complete the test two to three months after the training.
- Ensure that participants view this testing as a tool for evaluating the training, *not* the trainee.
- Apply the same post-course test to employees who did not attend the course but are responsible for similar results. Compare the results to the trainees' results.
- Create simulation exercises for trainees to apply newly learned techniques.
- Use a skill checklist to evaluate participants on a given skill.

Level Three: Behavior Change

- This phase assesses the trainee's application of new skills back on the job. This level of evaluation typically occurs about six months after training.
- Use 360-degree feedback to document observable changes.
- Use productivity reports or other data that relate directly to new skills to assess pre-course and post-course competence.
- Determine what kinds of incentives are in place to encourage the practice of newly learned techniques. If there are none, work with management to create conditions that encourage success.
- Determine what barriers might exist to practicing new techniques. Work with the management team to minimize or remove barriers before evaluating results.
- Consider what tools, resources, or equipment trainees need to use their new skills and evaluate changed behavior where optional conditions for success are in place.

Level Four: Achieving Quantifiable Results

- Results are quantifiable outcomes that were identified in the up-front analysis.

- The key question for this level of evaluation is: Has a problem been solved or a gap closed?
- The following are examples of changes that you're looking for:
  ✓ Fewer errors
  ✓ Increased customer satisfaction
  ✓ Reduced infractions of policies or standards
  ✓ Faster production time
- This phase of the evaluation process is similar to a cost-benefit analysis. Results are assessed in the context of the time and money invested in the training program and the length of time required to achieve the desired results.
- The time frame for measuring results after training is directly related to the size or extent of the problem or opportunity that the training addressed. The greater the changes required are, the longer the evaluation period is.
- As a general rule, results should be evaluated at least three months after training and by no later than twelve months. After twelve months, the conditions for success have usually changed significantly, and it becomes more difficult to measure results directly related to specific training initiatives.

Note

1. Donald Kirkpatrick, *Evaluating Training Programs,* 2nd ed. (San Francisco: Berrett-Koehler Publishers, 1998).

Measuring Training Results

> *"If you think that the cost of education is high,
> consider the price of ignorance."*
>
> —HENRY DAVID THOREAU
> Successful Pencil
> Manufacturer, Author,
> Poet, and Philosopher

Training needs and benefits are often described in anecdotal terms, but training dollars need to be justified like any other expenditure.

- To measure training results it is important to analyze:
  - ✓ The current competence level
  - ✓ The required competence level
  - ✓ Time frame for results
  - ✓ Costs of results
- Examples of current competency measures are:
  - ✓ Documented error rates
  - ✓ Time required completing specific tasks
  - ✓ Complaints from customers about delays or personal service attitudes
  - ✓ Complaints from staff about supervisory practices
  - ✓ Equipment malfunctions related to inexperience
  - ✓ Noncompliance or infractions of government policies
- Determining competence is not easy. These indicators can help managers to quantify competence levels:
  - ✓ Amount of time supervisors invest in coaching and monitoring employees
  - ✓ Employee likelihood to assume new tasks
  - ✓ Real business benefits of teamwork
  - ✓ Productivity figures that have changed significantly compared with results in previous years
  - ✓ Competitors' productivity figures
  - ✓ External benchmarks for similar processes
  - ✓ Employee attitude surveys and training needs analyses

✓ Observations and recommendations recorded in performance appraisals

✓ Opportunities to practice new skills

Competence is difficult to quantify for wide-scale training initiatives that focus on promoting large-scale change, such as organization-wide reengineering or the creation of a vision and mission. For these cases, identify one or two key outcomes that can be used as a reference for determining current competence levels.

Required Competence Levels

- The required level of competence will be expressed in the same quantifiable measurements as current competence levels.
- In order to establish realistic expectations, consider the following:
  ✓ Business-plan requirements. Are certain standards expected in order to meet the needs of customers?
  ✓ The degree of expertise an employee should demonstrate with little supervision.
  ✓ Internal and external customer expectations.
  ✓ The opportunity employees have to practice new skills or techniques.
  ✓ Incentives for employees to practice new skills or techniques.
  ✓ Potential barriers to effective performance of new skills, such as unclear operating procedures or poor equipment.

The Time Frame for Achieving Results

- Training results are not instantaneous. As a general rule of thumb, the greater the long-term impact of the training results, the longer the time frame for measuring results.
- The following guidelines can be used for setting meaningful time frames for measuring results:
  ✓ Regular reports that describe production and error rates: What is the typical period before noticing improvements?
  ✓ Operational requirements that specify important improvement deadlines.
  ✓ The period of time in which previous training resulted in meaningful improvements.

- Other conditions (tools, coaching, opportunity) that will have an impact on the use of new skills include:
  - ✓ The length of time participants have been in their current position
  - ✓ Costs for achieving meaningful results, including supervisory coaching time
  - ✓ The cost of the results of training over a period of time has multiple components, among them:
    - The costs of facilitation
    - Course design costs
    - Facilities costs
    - Materials costs (workbooks, videos, training aids)
    - Travel and accommodations costs for facilitators or trainees, or both
    - Time off the job for trainees (lost production time or missed opportunities)
    - Dedicated equipment for practice or experimentation
- The total cost of a training initiative should be assessed against the expected quantifiable results in order to derive a cost-benefit statement. If the costs exceed the expected benefits, determine which costs can be reduced.
- When looking at the big picture of training results, consider also the hidden factors that undermine results:
  - ✓ Lack of supervisory time to help staff implement new skills
  - ✓ Reassignment of newly trained employees to positions that do not require the use of recently learned skills
  - ✓ The introduction of new equipment or processes that makes new skills obsolete

Auditing the Training Function

At work and in play, we regularly evaluate what we do or what happens to us. Similarly, we need to regularly evaluate whether the resources we provide to develop our people are providing us with the benefits that they were designed to achieve. This can be done in-house, or by an outside consultant, should objectivity be an issue. This chapter provides the reasons for and methodology for evaluating your programs.

- Program evaluations in organizational settings are different in that they:
  ✓ Are usually carried out by a team after a proposal has been approved
  ✓ Attempt to achieve objectives that are agreed to by key stakeholders and can only be observed over time (that is, the difference among program objectives, implementation, and results)
  ✓ Have a formal reporting component at the end
- Program evaluations are a collection of methods, skills, and sensitivities necessary to determine whether a service:
  ✓ Is needed
  ✓ Is likely to be used
  ✓ Is sufficiently intensive to meet the unmet identified needs
  ✓ Is offered as planned
  ✓ Actually does help people
  ✓ Can improve the program

As such, program evaluations should be done as often as is practical to ensure that continuous improvement is built into the system.

The key to the success of any program evaluation is the planning process. Evaluators need to become familiar with the nature of the program, the people served, and the goals and structure of the program being evaluated. In addition, they must seek to learn why an evaluation is being considered. How is this done?

Step 1 requires that the researchers:

- Identify and meet with key stakeholders—all persons involved in or affected by the evaluation should be identified and listed so that their needs may be addressed.
- Establish clear program evaluation objectives by finding out:
  ✓ Who wants the evaluation?
  ✓ Why is an evaluation needed?
  ✓ What is the focus?
  ✓ What type is appropriate?

✓ How long do we have?
✓ What resources are available to support an evaluation?

Step 2 would see the researcher(s) create a sound design by:

- Obtaining a description of the program.
- Becoming familiar with the program by reviewing all literature, records, and so forth.
- Determining the methodology. This would include:
  ✓ Establishing a sample size that is large enough to ensure that the data gathered would be representative of the population so as to be valid and reliable.
  ✓ Deciding on the scope of the data collection. How much is enough? Collect only as much as will be necessary to meet your objectives.
  ✓ Selecting appropriate instruments. A variety of data collection methods ought to be employed in order to decrease the likelihood of error.
  ✓ Ensuring cost effectiveness. The evaluation should be efficient and produce information of sufficient value so that the resources expended can be justified. This includes ensuring that the evaluation's completion is planned within a reasonable and doable amount of time for data collection, analysis, and reporting.
- Presenting a proposal, preferably in writing outlining the previous items.
- Obtaining a formal written agreement outlining what is to be done, how, by whom, when, and for how much.

Step 3. Gather data effectively. The guidelines to follow include:

✓ Not becoming a data junkie. It is tempting to gather great amounts of data to analyze and interpret; however, strive to set reasonable expectations of data collection within your time frame and budget while obtaining only information that is essential. Ask yourself whether this information is interesting or if it is both interesting and essential to the program objectives. It is easy to get side-tracked. Keep your program objectives clearly in focus while you implement the evaluation.
✓ Keeping it simple and practical. Design your questions as practically as you can and your responses will be more useful. Before

you begin your evaluation, you should practice your interview, survey, and focus-group questions on an outside party to determine validity and refine your focus. This is an excellent way to iron out any awkward or confusing questions.

✓ Gathering, observing, recording, and measuring both qualitative and quantitative feedback from all key stakeholders. Systematically reviewing the information throughout the collection and analysis process to reveal any errors and to ensure that evaluation questions are being answered effectively.

Step 4. Evaluate the data:

✓ Be sure to apply recognized standards throughout the process of planning, conducting, and reporting evaluations.

✓ Review the data legally, ethically, and with due regard for the welfare of those involved in the evaluation as well as those affected by its results. The human rights of the participants must be protected and respected at all times. Participants must not feel threatened or harmed in any way throughout the evaluation process. Confidentiality and the security of the data collected must be ensured and upheld.

✓ Meet with key stakeholders regularly to maintain rapport and confidence, communicate findings and cross-check data for misunderstandings and reliability.

Step 5. Report the Findings:

✓ Final reports should clearly describe the program being evaluated, including the context (influences that may impact the program or historical information), the purposes and procedures (sources must be described in enough detail to ensure accuracy of assessment), and findings of the evaluation. The values, perspectives, procedures, and rationale used to interpret findings should be carefully described so that all biases for judgment criteria are clear and any conclusions reached in an evaluation are explicitly justified. Stakeholders can then assess the information fairly.

✓ Reports should encourage the likelihood of accessibility and follow-through by stakeholders and must be made in a timely, cost-effective, professional manner. Recommendations are best developed with stakeholders at the draft reporting stage and then later finalized for the report.

✓ Avoid writing a report that will gather dust and sit on a shelf because no one can read it. Few people will access your report, let alone understand it if that means arduously sifting through jargon and endless statistical analysis.

✓ Present your report in a practical mix of qualitative interpretation and quantitative analysis. Many people learn more effectively with visual aids such as graphs and charts.

✓ Don't get sidetracked with interesting but useless information in your report. Ensure that the evaluation will reveal and convey adequate information about the features that determine worth or merit of the program being evaluated.

✓ Tell the truth. There is often a tendency to please the paying customer and focus on favorable findings that may show little program impact and ignore the negative. Choosing to emphasize favorable information is appropriate at times but certainly not at the expense of the truth or to please the sponsors.

✓ Although program evaluations have an improvement focus, in the course of the evaluation mistakes and failures will become evident. And as much as the truth is painful, it is through our errors that we learn to improve and to change. Instead of hiding or condemning these findings, help to highlight recommendations that will address these important issues in a way that all stakeholders will understand and learn from. It is imperative for evaluators to encourage all stakeholders to approach the evaluation with an open mind throughout the entire process right through to the reporting stage.

✓ Effectively communicating results should include a combination of a personal oral presentation using some visual aids to demonstrate and highlight major findings while the final written document serves as an official record that includes details of the procedure, findings, and statistical analyses. No raw data is included in the final report.

Step 6. In conclusion:

✓ Monitoring can verify that an effective program remains so even after implementation and/or can isolate problems occurring when, for instance, the socio-political environment changes. It can take on a formative function in resolving identified issues and if resolution is untenable, monitoring can summarize as well.

Benchmarking

The process of benchmarking allows you to examine the effectiveness of the training process and programs by comparing them to an acknowledged standard in order to learn from the research and make meaningful improvements. It is a series of structured steps that probe *how* and *why* another process is effective, by collecting and investigating data, and interviewing key process owners.

- There are three kinds of benchmarking:
  1. *Specific:* comparing one unit or department within an organization
  2. *Generic:* comparing an organization to overall benchmarks (for industries, geographic areas, same-size organizations)
  3. *Competitive:* comparing an organization to one or two targeted organizations
- Increasingly, benchmarking training practices is ongoing to generate continuous improvements, to link training to business priorities, and to identify potential savings.
- Reasons for benchmarking can include:
  ✓ To set standards or adjust current standards; for example, the number of training days allocated per employee
  ✓ To link training to human resources' activities; for example, recruitment, selection, and performance evaluation
  ✓ To strengthen specific training processes; for example, needs analysis, gathering feedback, and realistic measures
  ✓ To align training with business planning; for example, budget parameters and executive support
- Benchmarking best practices in training can refer to:

✓ Organization-wide training practices and costs
✓ Training-department practices and costs
- Benchmarking organization-wide training practices and costs can examine:
  ✓ Annual training costs per employee
  ✓ Annual training days per employee
  ✓ Total annual training costs represented as a percentage of total annual salary costs
  ✓ Salaries of training-department staff represented as a percentage of total salaries in the organization
  ✓ Ratio of training-department staff to total staff
  ✓ Training evaluation and measurement tools
  ✓ Training planning and budgeting practices
- Training practices can be difficult to benchmark because organizations differ radically in their expectations for training. However, by identifying some key processes, comparing your practices to organizations with similar challenges, and following the seven key steps in benchmarking, you can bring a better business focus to your training.
- There are eight key steps for using benchmarking to improve your costs and effectiveness:
  1. Choose the processes to be benchmarked.
  2. Select and train the benchmarking team.
  3. Select the right partner.
  4. Analyze your own processes.
  5. Gather data from all appropriate sources.
  6. Identify the gaps between your processes and those recognized as "best practices."
  7. Develop a plan for improvement.
  8. Implement the required changes.

The following guidelines can be used to implement each of the key steps:

Step One: Choose Processes to Be Benchmarked.
  ✓ Interview key customer groups to understand what is important to them with respect to training outcomes.
  ✓ Analyze the major costs of your training department and training programs to the organization.

✓ Clarify the key goals and objectives for a training department in the overall organizational business plan.

✓ Prioritize one or two practices as areas for improvement.

✓ Identify specific improvements you hope to achieve.

Step Two: Select and Train the Benchmarking Team.

✓ Put together a cross-functional team with representatives from key customer groups.

✓ Include both management and nonmanagement representatives to give the team the advantage of different perspectives.

✓ Choose team members who are enthusiastic about change.

✓ Ensure that team members have a basic understanding of the processes being examined.

✓ Include a senior person, capable of authorizing changes.

Step Three: Select the Right Partner.

✓ Consider consulting firms that have databases on leading organizations and best practices.

✓ Consult with members of professional associations who might be able to identify leaders in the area you have chosen.

✓ Seek out those government agencies and industry associations who are willing to assist with your information gathering.

✓ Consider organizations of similar size as your benchmarks for training practices.

Step Four: Analyze Your Own Processes.

✓ Measure both inputs and outputs of a training process.

✓ Use factual data such as time, costs, and employee time.

✓ Use flowcharts to identify process components.

Step Five: Gather Data. If you conduct research through visits to other organizations:

✓ Get permission from a person in that organization with the necessary power to make such a decision.

✓ Be clear about the information you require and the time the visit will take. Have your team prepare a list of the information it is seeking.

✓ Offer reciprocal help and information in return for the organization's cooperation.

✓ Determine if your host organization is likely to charge a fee for sharing their "best practices."
✓ Gather additional information as may be required through:
  • Networking at conferences
  • Interviewing employees who have worked at these organizations previously
  • Trade associations
  • The Internet (home pages, chat groups)
  • Trade journals

Step Six: Identify Gaps.
  ✓ Compare "best practices" data with your organization's data.
  ✓ Determine which variables are within your control for effecting change.
  ✓ Clarify the benefits the organization will gain by closing the gap.

Step Seven: Develop a Plan for Improvement. Document an action plan that contains:
  ✓ The steps to be taken
  ✓ Who will need to be informed about the plan
  ✓ Who will be responsible for each step
  ✓ When each step will be completed

Step Eight: Implement the Required Changes.
  ✓ Set realistic deadlines for implementation.
  ✓ Develop a clear communication plan about the change implementation.
  ✓ Be very clear about the cooperation and approvals you require from others in your organization.
  ✓ Issue regular progress reports.
  ✓ Ask your customers to evaluate your results.

Be prepared to amend your plan as business conditions change.

IX

Developing Trainers and Facilitators

Train-the-Trainer Sessions

"Teachers open the door. You enter by yourself."

—CHINESE PROVERB

Whether you are an external training provider or an in-house training professional, from time to time, you may train others in the delivery of a training session in order to increase the pool of available trainers for key programs.

There are three important responsibilities for train-the-trainer sessions:

1. Selection of participants
2. Preparation of materials
3. Conducting the session

Selecting Participants

- Seek nominations from managers about staff who:
  - ✓ Have experience in presenting to groups
  - ✓ Have some knowledge in the subject area
  - ✓ Are regarded as champions
- Interview potential trainers to get a sense of their style and commitment to the project. It is better to disappoint one potential trainer than to disappoint trainees whose learning was compromised by a poor facilitator.
- Do not rule out nominees with no previous training experience. Consider other related experience, such as sales presentations, community relations, and experience in chairing meetings.

Preparing Materials

- A facilitator's binder should contain:
  - ✓ Complete participant's manual
  - ✓ Comprehensive facilitator notes
  - ✓ Guidelines and articles about effective facilitation techniques

✓ Complete set of overheads
✓ Complete set of handouts
✓ Copies of videos used during the training session
✓ Evaluation form used for the course
- In order to make the facilitator's guide user friendly:
  ✓ Use symbols to denote *flip chart, overhead, PowerPoint,* and *handouts* as they occur in the session.
  ✓ Use only the right-hand side of the manual for printed information. Leave the left-hand side blank for notes.
  ✓ Integrate copies of overheads and handouts as they occur during the session, so that users do not need to flip back and forth in the manual.
  ✓ Include suggested responses for all exercises. Make the list as comprehensive as possible.
  ✓ Include information and background data that will help facilitators deal with some potentially difficult teaching principles.
  ✓ Lay out the manual as attractively as possible, and use bold type so that the facilitator can see it easily at a comfortable distance.
  ✓ Use different colors to delineate the facilitator's role and the participants' activities.
  ✓ Use well-marked dividers for each separate lesson or exercise.

Conducting the Session

- Review the key teaching principles and anticipated outcomes informally with participants before walking them through the manual.
- Discuss the group's experiences as trainees (best and worst experiences) as an aid to understanding the trainees' perspectives.
- Review the manual and the lessons in digestible chunks, and debrief facilitators after each section.
- Conduct all role plays and exercises so that facilitators appreciate the impact these will have on trainees.
- Assign facilitators to deliver individual sections to the group after a comprehensive review of the manual. Allow them enough time to prepare the lesson plans and to rehearse.
- Be constructive in debriefing facilitators about delivery glitches.
- Debrief each facilitator in private about his or her facilitator style and technique.

- Videotape some practice sessions, and let facilitators review their own performances.
- Review evaluations from previous courses with the group to understand some major concerns and highlights of previous courses.
- Set up a hotline so that facilitators can contact you with urgent issues during a course they are conducting.
- Send updates, amendments, and tips to facilitators during the course delivery schedule.
- Prepare a list of facilitator names and contact details so they can share advice with each other after conducting the course solo.

Professional Development for Trainers and Facilitators

Trainers and facilitators themselves can benefit from ongoing skills development, feedback, and coaching. Internal leaders, external customers, and employees are redefining what they expect from training.

Here are some inexpensive ways to support and encourage professional development.

- Create mentoring partnerships between seasoned and less experienced trainers; focus on developing one or two specific training competencies.
- Set up learning forums with skilled presenters in the marketing, sales, and public relations departments.
- Invite training vendors and consultants to discuss effective training practices in other organizations they support.
- Convene a group of trainers to analyze feedback reports from key courses to set action plans to increase the satisfaction ratings.
- Create partnerships with training teams in your industry or community to share best practices and resource material.

- Obtain permission for trainers to audit courses in other organizations or local colleges to identify some effective techniques.
- Invite employees to a focus group to discuss good/bad facilitation techniques based on their experiences.
- Arrange for trainers to make presentations at events that are outside their normal activities and comfort zones—for example, orientation sessions, trade shows, or community events.
- Assign specific training topics to trainers who will develop and present a short course for other trainers, for example:
  - ✓ Handling difficult behavior
  - ✓ Time management in the classroom
  - ✓ Dealing with large groups
- Arrange opportunities for trainers to observe senior leaders present to groups; debrief with the trainers about their observations and lessons learned.
- Set up peer partnerships for trainers, who will observe each other in the classroom and give specific feedback on strengths and weaknesses.
- Align trainers more closely with the business plan by:
  - ✓ Visiting customer sites
  - ✓ Meeting with senior leaders
  - ✓ Shadowing an employee for a week to understand specific jobs in more detail
  - ✓ Facilitating team meetings in other parts of the organization
  - ✓ Designing and conducting a training needs analysis
- Work with local chapters of training or human resources associations to develop a training skills curriculum; offer to pilot the course at your organization in exchange for services and expertise.
- Partner with the local Toastmasters association to share techniques and tips.
- Offer training support services to a community organization that trains volunteers. (This will create goodwill for your organization while trainers practice skills in a different environment.)

Professional Associations: A Checklist for Selecting and Joining

Caveat Emptor ("Buyer Beware")

Professional associations keep trainers abreast of trends and help to develop contacts for sharing information. The number of associations is increasing as new training specializations emerge (for example, multimedia).

- The primary benefits of joining an association are:
  - ✓ Networking opportunities
  - ✓ Professional development
  - ✓ Access to up-to-date research
- Here are some guidelines in deciding which association(s) to join, especially if affordability is an issue. Talk to employees of the association itself, as well as with your professional colleagues, and establish the following:
  - ✓ Does membership entitle you to reduced conference fees? Are the discounts significant?
  - ✓ Does the association publish an annual member directory? This is an important networking tool.
  - ✓ Is there a local chapter?
  - ✓ Does the local chapter meet regularly, and if so, how often?
  - ✓ Do your professional colleagues recommend the association?
  - ✓ Does the association publish a regular newsletter or magazine?
  - ✓ Is the information the association provides relevant and interesting?
  - ✓ Is association information accessible on the Internet?
  - ✓ Does the association provide specialized research on request, for example, best practices, statistics, or case studies?
  - ✓ Has the membership base increased annually?
  - ✓ What percentage of members renews its membership annually?
  - ✓ Are participant evaluation summaries available from previous conferences and seminars?
  - ✓ Who is the executive director of the association, and what are his or her credentials?

✓ Who are the board members of the association?

✓ What is the profile of the membership base: their experience levels, industry groups, and so forth?

✓ Does the association set professional standards that are recognized in the industry?

✓ Does the association conduct certification programs that are recognized in the industry?

✓ Are you treated with courtesy when you call in person or on the telephone?

✓ Is there a resource center at the association office that members can use?

✓ Does membership entitle you to discounts on training videos and books?

✓ How does the cost of membership compare with other professional associations?

✓ How will joining a particular association support your own specific professional development interests?

- To reduce costs and maximize your opportunity to take advantage of multiple memberships, consider:

  ✓ Sharing a membership with others in your organization

  ✓ Exchanging association literature with colleagues who have joined other associations

  ✓ Using the Internet for information and advice

- Finally, if dollars are tight, consider forming an informal networking group. Assign research projects to members, exchange interesting articles, and share experiences.

X
Sustaining the Impact of Training

T he impact of training dollars can be significantly increased if conditions are created that encourage people to apply their learning back on the job. Part X examines the role of the line manager as a partner in this process.

Manager's Role in Supporting Training

"An organization attracts you to work there; only a manager inspires loyalty."

—KATHY CONWAY
Author of *The Trainer's Tool Kit*

Managers dispense rewards and punishments. They have more control over the behavior and performance of employees than anyone else. As such, their attitude toward learning and specific courses will have a major impact on whether skills are transferred back onto the job.

- Managers have three key roles vis-à-vis training for their team members:
  1. Recommending specific training courses or activities and linking them to the employee's role and performance measures
  2. Debriefing trainees on lessons learned and linking these lessons to specific activities and opportunities
  3. Conducting follow-up as new skills are applied through action plans and feedback
- A manager also has responsibilities to the organization in supporting training's overall effectiveness. These include:
  ✓ Recommending new or expanded training courses to meet business challenges
  ✓ Recommending training course content that reflects the day-to-day working environment, including case studies
  ✓ Providing realistic feedback about a course's objectives and effectiveness after trainees have practiced new skills on the job
- Here are other ways that managers can strengthen the link between training activities and organizational impact:
  ✓ Arrange for employees who have attended a training session to present a short overview of key lessons to the team.
  ✓ Set up a "lending library" of training course manuals and literature for team members to use as reference guides.
  ✓ Create a customized feedback form for returning trainees to complete that allows others on the team to prepare for the course or to consider attending it.

✓ Invite subject-matter experts to discuss some key lessons after a team has attended a course.

✓ Compile lists of course-related reading materials and resources that team members can reference after a course.

✓ Develop a code of conduct for the team that sets out expectations for appropriate behavior while attending training—for example, punctuality, cooperation, advance preparation, and so forth—which ensures that time-off-the-job is well spent.

✓ Nominate specific employees as post-course "coaches" who can assist recent trainees in applying new skills with confidence.

✓ Incorporate observations about an employee's post-course training outcomes into the annual performance review.

✓ Create specialized projects that allow employees to practice and assess new skills; solicit employee input about potential projects.

✓ Develop a post-training feedback agreement with individual employees that focuses on applying key training outcomes.

• A manager must strive to model new skills that employees learn in training. Managers should also point to others who practice a skill well, as effective role-modeling behavior. It is unlikely employees will apply new skills that are neither valued nor recognized.

Coaching for Skills Development

"The focus is on helping an employee become strong, not about making the employee feel better about being weak."

—CHIP BELL
Author of *Managers as Mentors*

The day-to-day interaction between the manager and employee will have an enormous impact on the performance and behavior of the employee. Having the manager act as a coach, using similar strategies used in effective teamwork outside of the workplace, is a useful starting point.

- Coaching for skills development is based on the same principles that underlie all effective coaching, specifically:
  - ✓ A formal or implied contract about the objective, and two-way expectations and boundaries
  - ✓ Observable behavior as a foundation for feedback
  - ✓ Feedback that balances positive reinforcement with suggestions for improvement
  - ✓ Opportunities for demonstration and practice
  - ✓ Setting clear success measures and standards
  - ✓ Balancing personal outcomes for the employee with organizational impact
- Managers coach for skill development to support formal training or on-the-job training. The coaching objective is to increase an employee's confidence and success in the current role or to prepare an employee for greater responsibilities in other roles.
- The following are benefits of one-on-one coaching for skills development:
  - ✓ Coaching is targeted to the employee's experience level and role with the organization.
  - ✓ Sessions can be conducted over time.
  - ✓ Assumptions can be tested and changed if necessary.
  - ✓ Employees can practice new skills immediately and receive prompt feedback.
  - ✓ Both parties can discuss their preferred feedback styles and can create a two-way feedback agreement.
  - ✓ Success can be recognized and celebrated immediately.
- Here are some coaching guidelines for managers:
  - ✓ Provide content from the business plan to the employee to show how the employee's work fits into the bigger picture.
  - ✓ Establish some visible measures for success when setting a plan to give you a baseline for your comments.
  - ✓ Solicit the employee's perspective on his/her current level of performance.
  - ✓ Use the opportunity to do some two-way brainstorming about practical assignments for applying new skills.
  - ✓ Use a combination of "open" and "closed" questions to steer the discussion.
  - ✓ Refer to the availability of specific internal courses when appropriate to support your one-on-one coaching.

✓ Solicit the employee's input about how to conduct a follow-up meeting and what feedback is required.

✓ Focus first on the desired outcome and then on the improvement when suggesting improvements.

✓ Identify others in the organization who provide role-modeling opportunities for the specific skills you are addressing.

✓ Be sure to address the *when* and *why* as well as the "how" and "what" in coaching sessions.

✓ Reward skill development with creative assignments that balance risk taking with confidence building.

✓ As employees master new skills, arrange for them to coach others to sustain and reinforce development.

Individual Development Plans

"If you want happiness for a year, inherit a fortune.
If you want happiness that lasts, help someone."

—UNKNOWN

An individual development plan is a formal contract between a manager and an employee that identifies specific development activities that link an employee's interest and skills to organizational need. Learning activities may be both formal and informal and can include self-directed activities, mentoring opportunities, and practical assignments.

• An individual development plan is predicated on two-way commitment:

  ✓ The employee's responsibility to do realistic self-assessment and research

  ✓ The manager's responsibility to create a forum for effective discussion and recommendations

• The plan is the outcome of one or more meetings that address:

  ✓ The employee's and manager's perspective on the employee's effectiveness in the current role

✓ Mutual suggestions for increasing impact in the current role
✓ The employee's longer-term career interests within the organization (typically a two-year view)
✓ The manager's perspective on preparing for future opportunities, including an overview of organizational priorities
✓ Mutual brainstorming about formal and informal learning activities and training to support success
✓ Agreements about timelines, suggested resources, feedback commitments, and "check-in" dates
• Benefits of Individual Development Plans:
  ✓ Employees benefit because:
    • The process emphasizes their own role in career self-management and that they benefit most when they commit time and energy to it.
    • They are responsible for reflecting on their interests, skills, and achievements and thus can better communicate these to managers and others.
    • They can self-identify for participation in satisfying assignments, special projects, and learning activities.
    • They can relate personal goals to the bigger picture of the organization's long-term business planning.
    • They can seek specialized feedback about specific development needs and interests.
    • They can connect, through the manager, with others in the organization who can provide career information and advice.
  ✓ Managers benefit because they can:
    • Share the responsibility for developmental planning with employees rather than assuming full responsibility
    • Get a clearer picture of employees' interests and goals and can relate those interests to new tasks and assignments
    • Energize and retain employees by facilitating opportunities for new challenges in their current roles as well as preparing employees for other roles
    • Conduct a more focused planning session since the employees are better prepared
    • Create roles for experienced staff to be mentors and/or informal trainers for less experienced staff
    • Create low-cost, customized learning opportunities through assignments

- Respond to employee-initiated requests for specialized feedback
✓ The organization benefits because:
  - Individual development-planning support is a competitive advantage in attracting and retaining employees and maximizing employee motivation and productivity.
  - There is more specific and accurate information about employees' interests and goals to assist with future resource planning and succession planning.
  - The organization can plan for and assign training dollars more realistically.
  - Developmental planning can create more effective networks within the organization of people seeking out others for advice and information.

Exhibit 9 and Exhibit 10 are two samples, either of which might be useful to document a development plan.

The Development Planning Meeting

A development planning meeting reinforces the critical link between a manager and an employee in planning for success.

- The manager has the benefit of day-to-day observation of an employee's capability. Furthermore, the manager has the advantage of the "bigger picture" of what the organization needs and values in building skill capability and is in a unique position to align this information with an employee's performance. What a manager may not know, however, is:
  ✓ What accomplishments an employee is proud of
  ✓ How an employee defines "success"
  ✓ What potential roles and opportunities excite and energize an employee

Exhibit 9. Individual development plan.

To be completed by the employee only

My primary goal for the next two years is:

Developmental Activities (to be undertaken on my own initiative)				Developmental Activities (to be undertaken with manager support)			
Activity	Priority			Activity	Priority		
1. _____	H	M	L	1. _____	H	M	L
2. _____	H	M	L	2. _____	H	M	L
3. _____	H	M	L	3. _____	H	M	L
4. _____	H	M	L	4. _____	H	M	L
5. _____	H	M	L	5. _____	H	M	L

My manager can assist my development by (list specific information, approvals, contacts your manager can arrange, etc., and tentative completion dates):

_____

_____

_____

Exhibit 10. Sample employee planning guide.

Goal	Purpose	Steps to Goal	Time Frame	Resources Needed	Can My Manager Assist My Development?	Future Related Goals
					☐ Yes ☐ No	
					☐ Yes ☐ No	
					☐ Yes ☐ No	
					☐ Yes ☐ No	

✓ An employee's learning style and preferred learning activities

✓ What specific feedback an employee wants and why

- A development meeting requires planning by both the manager and the employee. It can be conducted as a single meeting or over a period of time. Although the discussion style may be informal, it is a businesslike undertaking. Employees should do thoughtful planning and prepare an agenda to guide the discussion.

Manager Preparation

- Experience shows that managers everywhere often resist these kinds of meetings because they feel somewhat unarmed and unsure how to react to employee plans. So, here are some steps to prepare for a discussion. Remember, these meetings are critical for keeping people committed over the long term.

  ✓ Review the job profile—highlight what skills and responsibilities are critical to continuing success on the job.

  ✓ Consider recent coaching and performance.

  ✓ Jot down some thoughts about how the job is evolving and what is in overall business planning that can help the employee see his or her job in the larger picture.

  ✓ Consider how you could answer this question, if asked: "How can I do my job better?"

  ✓ Review the tools the participants have—highlight the kinds of information you'd like to know (asking questions is a great sign of respect!).

  ✓ Jot down a few observations about strengths, opportunities, and recent feedback.

  ✓ Rather than gathering unrelated feedback, make a note to ask employees in advance what kinds of feedback they want and why.

Key Considerations for Employee Development

- As a manager conducting this exercise, consider these issues:

  ✓ *Timeliness*—Over what period does an employee hope to achieve a specific objective?

✓ *Time Investment*—What can the employee realistically commit to development?

✓ *Learning Styles and Preferences*—What excites and energizes an employee?

✓ *Personal Motivators*—What has mattered most to an employee about his or her career with the organization?

✓ *Personal Ambitions*—What does an employee hope to gain from personal development?

✓ *Relevance*—Is the employee comfortable in describing ambitions that others may not share?

✓ *Organizational Support*—Does the employee feel confident that the organization looks for ways people can contribute more?

✓ *Personal History*—Has the employee already demonstrated some self-directed energy and investment in his or her personal career management?

✓ *Unique Attributes*—Does the employee have skills and/or experience that are not now being fully utilized?

Balancing Support for Current and Future Success

• Typically, managers know the depth of an employee's experience. All employees need to develop job-specific competencies to be successful on the job. However, over the longer term, employees and the organization gain when managers provide guidance and feedback about growing their roles.

• Here are guidelines for supporting employees at different stages of maturity in their roles:

✓ If an employee is still *developing* on-the-job competence, a manager should focus on ensuring that an employee is equipped to perform satisfactorily, with limited focus on developing career potential.

✓ If an employee is *competent* on the job, a manager should focus equally on equipping the employee to master the current job and to prepare for satisfying new challenges.

✓ If an employee has *mastered* the current job, the manager should focus largely on equipping the employee to grow his or her impact in the organization.

Making the Most of Development Planning Meetings

C oaching for individual development planning is a balancing relationship. Since the learner sets the agenda, your role is not to be unconditionally supportive nor a critic. Here are some practical reminders:

Do

- *Listen.* Often, enthusiastic coaches concentrate on passing on everything they know, rather than focusing on your employee's concerns.
- *Give Feedback.* Make sure that your feedback addresses not only facts but also perceptions that the employee may be demonstrating.
- *Provide Information and Options.* Do some research about an employee's interests; consider the meeting as an opportunity for some brainstorming and creative planning.
- *Correct—When Required.* Do not be afraid to provide information if the employee is clearly set on an ill-formed plan of action.

Don't

- *Give Advice.* Provide options for consideration instead.
- *Criticize.* Don't discount a plan of action; help the employee to understand what a potential outcome will look like—the business context and the risks.
- *Define Success in Your Own Terms.* Success today doesn't look like what it used to—understand that the employee's workplace personality and aspirations may not be similar to your own.

Listening

This sounds easier than it is. To support others we have to "hear what they say"—that is, listen for the underlying messages as well as the actual words. To do that we need to:

- Concentrate.
- Remove distractions (mental as well as physical—it is not enough just to divert phone calls if you allow your mind to remain on other matters).
- Let your employee finish statements (do not start planning your reply while the employee is still in the middle of a statement).
- Analyze what is being said in order to select the important parts.
- Check for understanding—everyone has different organizational references and assumptions.

Questioning

Questions are a particularly powerful tool in your meetings. Facilitate better exchanges by:

- Letting the employee set the agenda for the meeting
- Asking for permission to probe when required
- Avoiding asking questions that are too general, and therefore threatening (for example, "What are your career goals?"; "What do you expect from me?")
- Ensuring your body language communicates respect and interest to match your questions
- Taking notes, when required—this technique is another form of respect for the employee

Feedback

Everyone has some previous experience with feedback. Discover your employee's preferred style and interests in receiving feedback. Describe your own comfort level with giving feedback, and create a "feedback pact" for your partnership. Make the most of your feedback opportunities by:

- Asking permission to give frank feedback as required
- Noting that your perspective is one perspective and that your employee may seek other input for important issues
- Using feedback to reinforce positive behavior and activities as well as to confront some inappropriate actions and behavior

- Being prepared to listen to and probe any feedback you do receive—about yourself or the organization
- Assisting your employee in approaching others for feedback

Developmental Learning Activities

There are many theories on learning styles. The most common relate to being an auditory, visual, or kinesthetic (hands-on) learner. While people learn better and faster in one modality, most will benefit from a hands-on approach as it gives them the opportunity to practice new skills. As part of a development portfolio, each manager should include some practical learning activities.

- Hands-on learning opportunities should reflect:
  - ✓ An employee's perspective on his/her interests, skills, and needs
  - ✓ A manager's frank feedback on an employee's development potential
  - ✓ Two-way brainstorming about meaningful learning activities
  - ✓ Mutual commitments about follow-up, research, time off the job, and "checking in"
- The best choices for learning activities are those that:
  - ✓ Balance risk-taking with confidence
  - ✓ Match an employee's learning style and preferences
  - ✓ Are realistic in terms of gaining skills that can be easily applied
  - ✓ Benefit the organization as well as the employee
  - ✓ Require investment (that is, time, energy, and resourcefulness) from the employee
- A developmental learning activity has three key components:
  1. The learning outcome can be *described* (what it looks like, how it is measured).
  2. The learning outcome can be *demonstrated* (how, where, and why it is applied in day-to-day business).

3. The learning outcome can be *debriefed* (how comfortable the employee was in attempting a new skill, what went well).

- A manager is not wholly responsible for describing, demonstrating, and debriefing; the responsibility can be shared with other employees, subject-mater experts, and managers. The manager is, however, instrumental in creating links with others who can support the employee. These can include, as well, others outside the organization, such as:
  - ✓ Retired specialists
  - ✓ Customers
  - ✓ Industry and professional contacts
  - ✓ Members of community and civic organizations
- The specific learning activities in the employee's development plan should balance:
  - ✓ Self-directed learning and self-assessment
  - ✓ Direct coaching by others
  - ✓ Independent practice
  - ✓ Specific feedback
  - ✓ Opportunities to observe others
- Action plans need not be grandiose, expensive, or time consuming. Arrange for the employee to:
  - ✓ Facilitate a team meeting
  - ✓ Chair a cross-functional committee
  - ✓ Represent the organization at an industry or community event
  - ✓ Make a presentation about a subject in which he/she is uniquely qualified
  - ✓ Participate in hiring and selection interviews
  - ✓ Conduct a specialized research assignment
  - ✓ Train and orient new staff
  - ✓ Act as a mentor to a junior staff member
  - ✓ Develop a learning plan for being mentored by a senior leader
  - ✓ Coordinate a staff conference or customer event
  - ✓ Meet with internal and external customers to gather specific feedback
  - ✓ Attend meetings at other levels or in other areas of the organization to act as scribe
  - ✓ Read and summarize the key points in a topical business book or report
  - ✓ Condense the key teaching points in a formal course to present to other team members

✓ Write an article for a business publication or staff newspaper
✓ Conduct a training needs analysis for your team
✓ Arrange a field trip to a customer's premises or an equipment supplier
✓ Act as a manager in your absence, or in another area
✓ Shadow an employee at a more senior level and record observations
✓ Practice operating a piece of equipment under the guidance of an expert
✓ Audit a training course at a more senior level
✓ Participate in an in-house focus group

Many more possibilities will emerge during discussion and as the plan evolves.

- A manager should remember to link learning activities and outcomes to the "bigger picture" of the organization's business by:
  ✓ Relating a new skill to a quality or service measure
  ✓ Relating a new assignment to specific job content
  ✓ Demonstrating how a skill or new experience will enhance personal confidence
  ✓ Identifying how an activity relates to a specific business plan objective
  ✓ Describing new skills in the context of expected behaviors or core competencies
  ✓ Recognizing new skills in the annual performance evaluation

XI
Growing Organization Capacity

P art XI provides insight into other state-of-the-art strategies for developing people outside of traditional training programs. It provides some practical tools for engaging and developing high performers though mentoring, succession planning, and career planning.

Mentoring Best Practices

> *"In training we try to make people fit better.
> With mentoring, we try to make fit people even
> better."*
>
> —KATHY CONWAY
> Author of *The Trainer's Tool Kit*

Mentoring is a customized development opportunity whereby an employee has access to the perspective and wisdom of a more seasoned employee. This partnership facilitates the ability of the mentee to contribute to the organization. A facilitated program typically links people who may not normally interact.

The advantage of implementing a mentoring program today is that we gain insight by researching what other organizations have done well. Here are some lessons learned.

- Mentoring works best when:
  - ✓ Organizations define what they expect from a mentoring program.
  - ✓ Organizations acknowledge that informal mentoring already goes on (thereby including, rather than excluding, those practicing it successfully).
  - ✓ Organizations create partnerships or employees with different, not similar, functional expertise (thereby not duplicating or jeopardizing manager-employee relationships).
  - ✓ Mentoring is targeted at high-performing individuals; it is not a remedial initiative.
  - ✓ Mentoring supports a career-development ethic that encourages the individual to manage his or her own career.
  - ✓ Mentees work hard on setting goals and taking equal responsibility for the success of the relationship.
  - ✓ Mentors view the process as an opportunity to practice and enhance leadership skills.
  - ✓ Mentors and mentees set up their own networking forums with each other to exchange ideas and successes.
  - ✓ Mentors gain something from the partnership—for example, enhanced leadership skills.

✓ There is an administrative infrastructure and someone who "checks in" on the progress of the relationship and is able to intervene if the process is not productive.

✓ There is clear differentiation between reporting relationships and mentoring relationships.

✓ The organization provides lots of tools, but encourages creativity and individuality in partnerships.

✓ Mentees don't expect promotions as an outcome; instead, participants will be more motivated to personalize development and explore more options.

✓ Participants expect the partnership to have highs and lows, and have contingency plans for the low time.

The following important shifts are from previous years:

Old Style	New Style
Mentors can aid the mentee best when the mentee has similar perceptions about the organization.	Mentees grow best by partnering with someone with a different perspective or career path.
Mentoring partners are most effective when they work in the same functional area.	Mentoring partners gain when they focus on common organizational skills for success, not functional expertise.
Mentors measure mentees' success by their *advancement* within the organization.	Mentors measure mentees' success by their *attachment* to the organization.
Mentoring partnerships rely on effective two-way interpersonal chemistry.	Mentoring partnerships rely on effective two-way respect and commitment.
Mentors help mentees to become more motivated.	Mentors help motivated people to become more effective.
Mentors have been consistently successful in their careers.	Mentors can provide insight on successes and failures—and allow mentees to learn from both.

Mentors coach mentees for *outcomes.*

Mentors coach mentees for *opportunities.*

Mentors rely on their own experience and expertise to help mentees.

Mentors rely on their network to help mentees.

Questions to Determine if Your Organization's Program Is Likely to be Successful

- Is leadership development an important component of the organizational strategy?   Yes   No

- Do you have a career self-management ethic that emphasizes individual accountability?   Yes   No

- Are self-service learning tools available (including tuition reimbursement)?   Yes   No

- Is accountability for employee performance a shared responsibility between HR and the senior team?   Yes   No

- Are coaching and feedback integral to a manager's job?   Yes   No

- Is staff retention a priority?   Yes   No

- Have common skills for success been identified (that is, core competencies, success dimensions, and so forth)?   Yes   No

- Are there some recognized role models and informal mentors within the organization?   Yes   No

- Would leaders and managers themselves benefit from practicing and demonstrating leadership by becoming formal mentors?   Yes   No

- Do you have the resources to train mentors and mentees prior to their involvement in the process?   Yes   No

Not all answers need to be yes; however, too few yes answers may indicate a need to reinforce some elements of your people-

. development strategy concurrent with the introduction of a mentoring program.

Implementing a Mentoring Program

"Success breeds success."

—UNKNOWN

Mentoring programs are a powerful strategy for developing talent by encouraging individuals to take responsibility for their long-term development. At the same time, mentors can increase their coaching, feedback, and leadership skills. The organization also benefits from more motivated, competent employees, less turnover, increased confidence and enthusiasm. In a nutshell, everyone benefits.

- The following guidelines were suggested by organizations that have implemented successful mentoring programs:
  - ✓ Set budget guidelines for the program since there will be costs for orientation sessions, self-assessment guides, and program publicity. Include the hidden costs of a program (for example, time off the job or travel costs).
  - ✓ Determine who can participate in the program as mentors and mentees, and the length of the program.
  - ✓ Decide whether the relationships will be one-on-one or involve more than one mentee per mentor.
  - ✓ Consider how the matching will be done after researching successful mentoring programs.
  - ✓ Set time limits for evaluating results. Experience suggests that one year is the optimum time frame for evaluating results.
  - ✓ Mentors should be at least two levels higher than a mentee so mentees have the advantage of senior perspective.
  - ✓ Develop a workbook or seminar that allows mentees to do a comprehensive self-assessment about goals, as well as their individual strengths and weaknesses.

✓ Provide the mentor and mentee with the tools to be able to establish an effective working relationship. This "contract" will include items such as:
  • Openness and honesty
  • A process for evaluation
  • Do's and don'ts during meetings
  • Confidentiality
  • Goals and objectives
  • Issues that will be off limits
  • Reasons for postponing or canceling meetings
  • Times, places, and frequency of meetings
• Determine appropriate recognition and incentives for mentors (for example, a Mentor of the Year award).
• Provide forums for mentors to meet with each other for sharing suggestions and successes. Do the same for mentees.
• Be sure to publicize successes and outcomes to keep the momentum strong.
• Recruit your highest potential performers as mentees. These are people who can do the following:
  ✓ Become a full partner in the relationship with the mentor.
  ✓ Establish a small number of long-term goals that are specific, measurable, achievable, realistic, and time based.
  ✓ Develop a plan to achieve long-term goals and dates by when they will be complete.
  ✓ Make a public commitment to their goals, so that others can monitor and encourage the mentee.
  ✓ Take ownership for goal achievement.
  ✓ Relish the opportunity to learn from others.
  ✓ Do one thing each day that will take them closer to their goal.
  ✓ Set goals that are important to them, as much as they may please others.
  ✓ Treat failure as an opportunity to learn.
  ✓ Keep track of the most important lessons learned so that they can be referred to in order to reinforce continuous learning.
  ✓ Learn to listen to and accept negative feedback as an opportunity to learn.
  ✓ Keep their goals in front of them constantly—for example, posted on a mirror at home or in a desk drawer.
  ✓ Approach each day with a sense of discovery.
  ✓ Take more risks.

✓ Keep a list of things that it would be good to learn within five, ten, and twenty years.
- Mentors can contribute to the development process in many different ways, including:
  ✓ Allowing the mentee to observe senior management meetings
  ✓ Taking the mentee to professional networking meetings
  ✓ Reviewing the mentees' résumé for critical comment
  ✓ Passing on topical articles and books for comment
  ✓ Discussing the impact of their own role models and mentors
  ✓ Passing on invitations to professional-development events such as breakfast meetings and product launches
- Mentoring meetings are most successful when they follow a set format:
  ✓ Updates on action items
  ✓ Debriefing on problematic assignments since the last meeting
  ✓ Feedback by the mentor on his or her observations of the mentee in action
  ✓ Suggestion for development initiatives, including reading and industry events
  ✓ Opportunity for the mentee to share success stories
  ✓ Mutual "homework" assignments that cover both research and action items
- Regular meetings between mentor and mentee will be productive if:
  ✓ There is a focus on one area of development.
  ✓ The meeting ends with "homework" assignments, and these are documented. The assignments are specific, with timelines and methods agreed upon.
  ✓ Both sides practice careful listening.
  ✓ Time restrictions are honored.

Training and Orientation for Mentors and Mentees

"There's always room at the top."

—DANIEL WEBSTER
Statesman, Lawyer, and Orator

An orientation training session is an important step in launching successful partnerships. These sessions create opportunities to probe expectations, including potential challenges, review organizational support for the program, and establish a network for participants.

- Sessions are typically held separately for mentors and mentees, as each group may feel constrained in asking questions in front of their potential partners. Separate sessions will also reinforce the networking and learning opportunities that each group has for sharing suggestions and techniques. Effective orientation sessions combine elements of:
  ✓ Information
  ✓ Advice from others
  ✓ Practice exercises and case studies
  ✓ Workbooks and guidelines
  ✓ Sufficient time for questions and answers
- Here are some recommended components of mentoring orientation sessions (which are often summarized in a workbook or tool kit):

Organizational Support

✓ How the organization defines mentoring and its expected outcomes
✓ Program facilitator and his/her roles and responsibilities, including trouble-shooting
✓ Additional resources available (for example, communication-skills classes, names of previous participants, or self-assessment tools)
✓ Success measures both for the program and for individual partnerships

✓ Anticipated time commitments for meetings and other related activities (including guidelines for investing one's personal time)
✓ Scheduled check-ins and networking events to assess how partnerships are proceeding

Partnership Dynamics

✓ How participants were chosen
✓ How partners are matched
✓ Anticipated common outcomes balanced with partnerships' independence to set individual operating guidelines
✓ Partnership agreements that include discussions and commitments about confidentiality, honoring time commitments, learning styles, and personal expectations
✓ Addressing potential partnership breakdowns, including troubleshooting and replacing partnerships required (for example, transfers or overwhelming time commitments)
✓ How to be a responsible partner
✓ Concluding the partnership

Advice from Others

✓ Do's and don'ts from other organizations
✓ Advice from previous participants
✓ "Best practices" research
✓ Recommended reading, including articles
✓ Suggestions from recognized role models and mentors within the organization

Goal Setting

✓ How to set personal development expectations (for example, feedback or career self-management steps)
✓ Setting realistic expectations
✓ Roles and responsibilities within the partnership for goal setting
✓ Elements of a personal development plan
✓ Setting personal benchmarks for success
✓ Identifying potential activities that can support mentee goals (for example, internal meetings, networking groups, committee work, or related courses)

✓ Recalibrating goals as required
✓ Celebrating success

Communication Skills and Techniques

✓ Effective questioning skills
✓ Effective listening skills
✓ Seeking feedback
✓ Giving feedback
✓ Probing assumptions and observations
✓ Collaborative decision making and brainstorming techniques
✓ Personal style assessments
✓ Networking dynamics

Program Conclusion

✓ Summarizing outcomes
✓ Acknowledging a partner's contribution
✓ Feedback to the organization
✓ Personal action plan development
✓ Guidelines for keeping in touch with a partner
✓ Applying lessons learned on the job

Career Planning Programs

The training investment that organizations make is maximized when employees can link their own goals to business goals.

- Career development for employees in an organization can take many forms:
  ✓ Increased responsibility and enhanced skill sets in a current job
  ✓ A lateral move to another position
  ✓ Advancement to a higher level
  ✓ Long-term planning for a career change

- ✓ Reduced responsibilities for lifestyle priorities
- ✓ Retraining for new and emerging occupations
- Organizations that establish a clear relationship between training and career development enjoy the following benefits:
  - ✓ A competitive advantage in attracting new employees
  - ✓ A better ability to retain employees
  - ✓ Increased employee morale and motivation
  - ✓ Meaningful succession planning
  - ✓ Business plans that identify realistic objectives for employee development
- Here are some of the most common ways organizations promote individual responsibility for career planning:
  - ✓ The provision of standardized career planning seminars available to all employees—either mandatory or voluntary attendance, during or outside normal business hours
  - ✓ Career planning workbooks for use during seminars or as stand-alone aids
  - ✓ Self-help books, videos, or computer-based tools for self-directed study
  - ✓ The establishment of a formal mentor program with clear roles and responsibilities for both mentors and mentees
- An effective career planning seminar, workbook, or computer-based training aid should address the following elements:
  - ✓ Emphasis on individual accountability for career management
  - ✓ Up-to-date information about the competitive marketplace and the customer base
  - ✓ Self-assessment exercises about skills and personal preferences
  - ✓ Personal marketing techniques
  - ✓ Information-gathering techniques
  - ✓ Developing mentor relationships
  - ✓ Comprehensive information about in-house training
  - ✓ The relationship of continuous learning to corporate objectives
  - ✓ The importance of identifying hidden success factors: adapting to change, coping with stress, and helping others be successful
  - ✓ Cost-effectiveness
  - ✓ Accessibility for all employees, including employees at different geographic locations and those who work shifts
- Career planning programs work best when:
  - ✓ Senior management supports the program.

✓ There is a role for managers to support and reinforce the objectives of the program.

✓ There are self-study tools for employees to use for their personal development and growth.

Promoting Career Self-Management

The days of organizations throwing money at training are over. So too are the days when a manager took responsibility for the careers of his or her staff. Today, employees need to be proactive in taking charge of their learning and careers. They are the senior partners and their manager is the guide and facilitator.

- Visible support for individual career planning initiatives is becoming an increasingly important component of an organization's training strategy because it:
  ✓ Facilitates the process whereby individuals translate self-discovery into meaningful development activities
  ✓ Equips individuals to be proactive in finding ways to utilize skills gained from training courses
  ✓ Encourages individuals to link their strengths and interests to real and potential opportunities
- An organization can support a career self-management culture in many ways, including the following:
  ✓ Assigning clear roles and responsibilities for managers, employees, and the senior team to support development
  ✓ Providing facilitated sessions for voluntary employee participation
  ✓ Providing a variety of self-assessment tools and resources
  ✓ Training and coaching managers to be career development advocates for their staff
  ✓ Seeking input from employees about barriers to effective self-development and addressing these barriers

✓ Providing guidelines for individual development contracts between managers and employees

✓ Encouraging informational interviews as a learning tool and developing guidelines for conducting them

✓ Posting inventories of assignments and opportunities for interested employees to learn or practice new skills

✓ Posting lists of subject-matter experts within the organization
who are available for some one-on-one coaching

✓ Convening panels of leaders who describe their own career decisions and related activities

✓ Advertising all informal training with the organization, including "lunch and learns"

✓ Holding "open houses" in various departments to discuss job
content and qualifications

✓ Maintaining up-to-date lists of job specifications and experience
requirements that employees can access

✓ Holding open forums periodically to talk about what an organization will look like, and need, in a three- to five-year view

✓ Recognizing and rewarding effective coaches, role models, and
mentors

✓ Linking mentoring opportunities to pending skills shortages

✓ Creating mentoring opportunities for those who have taken the
initiative in personal career self-management

✓ Providing multiple examples of what core competencies "look"
like in everyday practice, together with practical suggestions for
activities that develop them

✓ Linking training courses to specific positions and roles within
the organization by listing these in course descriptions

✓ Canvassing participants in career planning sessions for suggestions for a training course curriculum

✓ Developing a Q&A on the organization's intranet for practical
career planning advice

✓ Equipping employees with skills that support career self-
management—for example, seeking feedback, conducting research, and effective networking

Succession Planning

D ownsizing, rightsizing, and reengineering have all had a devastating impact on the number of middle managers now available to step up to the plate and replace top managers as they come due for retirement. Succession planning helps to replace the talent that has dwindled following layoffs, resignations, transfers, or promotions. At the same time, it will grow the pool of people interested in other opportunities.

- There are seven important steps in creating effective succession:
  1. Identify the key corporate positions that are fundamental to the organization's success.
  2. Nominate high-performing individuals as potential successors. This is often done through succession planning committees with senior representatives of line functions, human resources staff, and training professionals.
  3. Assess key gaps in successors' skills to meet current and future requirements.
  4. Develop a comprehensive training strategy for successors that encompasses both formal and informal training.
  5. Identify and evaluate the training courses and options available that best suit your specific requirements.
  6. Calculate the costs of succession training and create a budget.
  7. Implement the succession-training plan by identifying key steps, deadlines, and measurement criteria.
- Important steps to develop successors include:

Assess Key Gaps in Successors' Skills

✓ Interview incumbents of key corporate positions to understand:
  - Their background and training
  - Their assessment of future skill requirements
  - The timeliness of developing effective successors
  - Their recommendations for effective successor training
  - Their availability to act as coaches and mentors to successors
  - Their assessment of successors' strengths and weaknesses
✓ Interview identified successors to understand their:

- Training and experience
- Self-assessment of skills needed in a more senior job
- Availability for long-term training
- Recommendations for effective succession training
- Short-term professional development plans

Identify Skills Gaps Under These Headings

✓ Business skills
✓ Industry-specific skills
✓ Management skills
   - Prioritize the importance of the skill gaps.
   - Secure agreement with incumbents and successors about time frames to address skill gaps.

Determine the Best Training Vehicle to Meet Skill Gaps

✓ Formal training
✓ On-the-job training
✓ Internal courses
✓ External courses
✓ Professional upgrading
✓ Job rotation
✓ Job shadowing
✓ Computer-based training
✓ Subscriptions to professional journals
✓ Task assignment to task forces
✓ Special projects
✓ Formal coaching or mentor contracts
✓ Educational upgrading
✓ Interorganizational exchange programs

Identify and Evaluate Training Courses for Successors

✓ Consult the in-house training catalog for available courses.
✓ Determine prices, availability, and waiting lists for external courses.
✓ Check references for external courses by contacting previous attendees.
✓ Develop "learning contracts" for informal training, coaching, or mentoring relationships.

✓ Ensure that succession candidates meet prerequisites for external courses, university programs, or professional upgrading.
✓ Consider a customized in-house program for succession candidates with common skill gaps.

Calculate Costs and Create a Budget

A budget for succession training includes:

✓ Course costs
✓ Travel and accommodation costs for out-of-town courses
✓ Subscriptions to professional journals
✓ Specialized equipment needs (for example, CD-ROM, Internet access, or interactive video learning facilities)
✓ The costs of time off the job

Implement the Succession Training Strategy

✓ Set deadlines for training that addresses high-priority gaps.
✓ Review the training plan annually to ensure it continues to meet business needs.
✓ Adapt the plan annually to meet new and emerging corporate priorities.
✓ Confirm budget approval for succession training costs annually. This is particularly important for long-term strategies.
✓ Set formal feedback guidelines for coaches and mentors to monitor progress and make recommendations.
✓ Create opportunities for succession candidates to practice and implement new skills.
✓ Keep abreast of new courses and lower-cost training options, and amend the training plan accordingly.
✓ Involve succession candidates in realistic self-assessment exercises after each important training component.
✓ Determine key learning outcomes for each training component, and monitor these outcomes rigorously.

Designing an In-House Succession Program

H aving a succession plan that is always current sends a signal to all would-be leaders that the organization is serious about maintaining the strength of its talent. An organization that plans for staff development will more than likely retain staff longer.

- Many organizations typically outsource the leadership development of the senior talent pool to established executive preparation programs at universities and other institutions. There are some disadvantages to this strategy:
  - ✓ These programs are typically expensive, often costing $10,000 or more.
  - ✓ The programs are not customized to your unique operating environment.
  - ✓ The programs cover a broad range of topics—not all of which are targeted to your candidate's or your organization's needs.
  - ✓ The learning is condensed into a short period of time.
  - ✓ There is no real opportunity for your candidate to practice newly acquired skills in case studies that reflect his or her workplace.
  - ✓ It is difficult for a candidate's manager to debrief the candidate after the program to set up a learning action plan.
  - ✓ There is the risk that recruiters will target your candidate for job search opportunities.
- To create realistic learning plan for a senior talent pool, consider the following:
  - ✓ Establishing a time frame for the learning experience—for example, twelve months
  - ✓ Establishing criteria for inclusion in the pool (for example, executive recommendation, performance and evaluation results, or candidate interest)
  - ✓ Designating key executive champions who will implement the strategy and monitor results
  - ✓ Determining realistic outcomes (for example, four or five candidates who can assume greater responsibility after twelve months)

- Recommended learning activities for potential leaders include:
  - ✓ *Competitive Intelligence.* Assign groups of three or four candidates to assess the strengths and weaknesses of some key competitors. Set a deadline for presentations to the senior team—for example, two months. The senior team will provide feedback and comments after each presentation.

    Outcomes

    - Teamwork dynamics
    - Presentation experience at the senior level
    - Opportunity to gain feedback from the senior team
    - Opportunity to probe and understand the competitive landscape
    - Experience in research and analysis techniques

  - ✓ *Brainstorming and Problem Solving.* Select three or four issues unique to your organization for the candidate pool to discuss and offer recommendations. Create an ongoing forum for the pool to meet with the senior executive for an effective exchange of ideas and solutions. These issues may be business-based or human resources based—for example, morale.

    Outcomes

    - Experience in interacting with senior team and/or senior executive that is atypical of normal meetings
    - Generates creative thinking and risk taking
    - Creates confidence in making recommendations and demonstrating reasoning and logic
    - Encourages effective listening and feedback when discussing ideas with others

  - ✓ *Executive Book Club.* Participants each design a reading list for themselves around key leadership and practical business issues by reading reviews of topical business books. Participants then prepare short summaries of books read for distribution to the executive team and the other participants. Participants and the senior team meet occasionally to discuss some key information from current books and assess their applicability to the organization.

Outcomes

- Participants and the executive team keep abreast of current organizational literature and engender an ongoing reading culture
- Participants develop an ability to assess a significant amount of data and identifying key points
- Improved presentation skills

✓ *Meeting with a Role Model.* Each participant identifies a business leader with whom he or she would like to meet. This involves research and reflection by each participant and emphasizes the importance of success models in sustaining high performance. The executive team utilizes its networks and contacts to arrange these meetings.

Outcomes

- The executive team will have put their combined networks to use and will have created a unique retention strategy by facilitating these meetings.
- Participants will learn to create an agenda for this meeting to maximize time and information.
- Participants will have gained both energy and insight from these individual meetings and an opportunity to present an overview to others in the organization.

- There are many other opportunities for creating a learning curriculum to meet succession needs—for example, mentoring or community service—together with your established training courses. The following benefits come from creating an in-house program:
  - ✓ The senior team has an opportunity to see candidates regularly and influence their development.
  - ✓ The senior team can take advantage of the specialized research candidates complete and recommendations presented.
  - ✓ The talent pool establishes networks that may not occur naturally.
  - ✓ The candidates' commitment to the organization strengthens as they see a bigger picture of the real business of the organization.
  - ✓ Time commitments and expenses are reduced significantly.
  - ✓ It will be easier to monitor those staff members who embrace this opportunity to learn as compared with those that consider new learning as a waste of time.

Ten Ways to Take the "Success" out of Succession Planning

E xecutives and employees alike often disparage the lack of visible and effective results in the organization's succession planning process. This holds true whether the process is formal or casual, highly transparent or secretive.

The following ten common mistakes can undermine results:

1. *Delegating Full Responsibility to Human Resources.* The executive team is ultimately responsible to all stakeholders for the ongoing health of the organization. HR can be a facilitator, providing intelligence about best practices and employee skills and interests, but it cannot commit the organization's resources to the task, nor assess the emerging business challenges that create successor profiles.

2. *Focusing Only on the Senior Team.* A senior team is mobile by definition, as its members are highly visible to competitors. Realistic plans must also include key groups and positions that are fundamental to your success and not easily replaced internally or accessed on the open market. These positions may be buried deep in the classification structure, but are no less critical to continuing success.

3. *Replacing People, Rather Than Developing Them.* A plan that simply identifies drop-dead successors typically overlooks the broader talent base available and may not be addressing fundamental changes in the competitive landscape. It is important to invest in all high performers who have the opportunity to grow organizational capacity.

4. *Not Consulting with Potential Successors.* More that a few organizations have been shocked when a top succession candidate has left the organization for a better opportunity, completely unaware of the plans for him or her. It's vital that succession candidates have an opportunity to discuss their development interest and goals to create a realistic action plan that excites them.

5. *Identifying Successors at Every Level.* A master chart that identifies likely successors for too many positions and levels within the organization drains energy from an organization. Employees need to feel some organizational "breathing space" to grow skills and to be recognized for future opportunities.

6. *Making Assumptions.* Not all people equipped to advance to the next level actually want to do so. Not all key jobs are fully understood by potential successors. Success depends on frank conversations as much as on detailed skill profiles.

7. *Not Updating Plans Regularly.* An annual plan typically doesn't reflect ongoing intelligence about business dynamics and employee achievements. Refine the plans as often as a senior team meets.

8. *Relying Exclusively on an Incumbent's Perspective.* An incumbent is one of many who should scope out position requirements and a successor profile. Internal and external clients, direct reports, and the senior team all have important insights about creating this profile.

9. *Outsourcing Successor Development.* Successor development cannot be done wholly off-site. The key ingredients of a plan involve internal exposure and experience, direct client contact, industry events and mentoring by key decision makers and role models. External courses can supplement, but not replace, your unique requirements.

10. *Calling the Recruiters Too Late.* The time to place a call for a key search is well in advance of a vacancy. Develop ongoing relationships with recruiters that specify target organizations and identify unique skills and emerging needs. Create opportunities for recruiters to understand your business thoroughly. Your search, when activated, will be more comprehensive.

Energizing High Performers Through Training and Learning Opportunities

Too often, the target audiences for training courses and limited training dollars are employees who underperform. Overlooked, often, are the loyal and skilled employees responsible for an organization's past and continuing success. It is important to invest in their continuing development and morale, as it is their energy and attitude that set the standards for others.

Here are some guidelines for creating informal learning opportunities that engage high-performing employees and expand their impact in the workplace:

- Through discussion, find out what achievements an employee is proud of and what assignments he or she has found most satisfying. Use the information to create new assignments that bring a balance of risk and energy to his/her role. We often know what employees have done, but not what they love to do! This allows an employee to practice his or her strengths in new or unusual circumstances.

Examples of Assignments

✓ An external assignment or exchange
✓ An opportunity to represent the organization within the community—for example, service club, schools, or industry associations
✓ Coordinating a conference for customers or a business unit
✓ Participation in hiring and recruitment

- Utilize the organization's networks and profile to create an opportunity for the employee to serve in a high-profile or executive role in an industry or professional association. Performers gain enhanced networks as well as the opportunity to develop influencing and leadership skills.

Examples of External Organizations

✓ Charitable organizations that the organization supports
✓ Advisory boards for specific courses at colleges and universities

✓ Civic organizations and service clubs
✓ Bodies that set industry standards
✓ Consumer groups linked to your industry

- Learn more about the employee's business role models and others he or she would enjoy meeting. Set up meetings for the employee with as many people as possible or facilitate a mentoring partnership. The employee gets interaction skills as well as valuable insights, which he or she can subsequently communicate to others.

Examples of Role Models

✓ Senior executives
✓ Key customers
✓ Retired executives
✓ Stock analysts and business writers
✓ University faculty members
✓ Local government leaders

- Personalize a training opportunity for the employee by sending him or her to a unique course that develops a specific interest area not normally offered through a traditional training curriculum. These courses are energizing for an employee and typically can create opportunities for the employee to present short presentations to others after the course that sharpen training and delivery skills.

Examples of Unique Courses

✓ Comedy workshops
✓ Specialized cooking courses
✓ Motivational speakers
✓ Arts and crafts
✓ Home repair and decorating
✓ Personal effectiveness skills (for example, speaking, writing, or managing time)
✓ Managing difficult people

- Establish a personal board of directors for an employee to review his or her personal career planning and development action plan. Draw on a variety of senior personnel to give pragmatic feedback and practical advice for longer-term development. This team can meet two or three times in a year to track development activities and create customized learning opportunities.

Examples of Advisory Meeting Topics

✓ Self-directed learning materials, including current business books
✓ Creating and sustaining networks
✓ Accessing a senior-level mentor
✓ Gathering meaningful feedback
✓ Setting goals, timelines, and measurements in a personal development planning process
✓ Balancing home and work

- There are many other learning opportunities that can be personally rewarding for high performers and use few training dollars. After the employee has completed a learning assignment, be sure to debrief the employee about new skills acquisition and create an action plan for expanding these skills in his or her ongoing role.

Index

Made in the USA
Lexington, KY
17 September 2016